# A 40-Day Journey to Your New Identity in Christ

RANDY VALENTINE

ISBN: 978-1-7361221-3-6
EBook: ISBN: 978-1-7361221-2-9

Cover design by: Nathan Valentine
Editing assistance by: Zachary Valentine

Printed in the United States of America

Third edition.

# TABLE OF CONTENTS

# DEDICATION

To everyone who is searching for freedom in life.
May God guide you into all Truth.

Welcome!

Ask yourself a simple question: Who am I? Your answer to that question will reveal your identity sources, and it will most likely reveal a lot about the purpose, or lack thereof, in your life. I have been on a journey to uncover the true meaning of life for quite some time. After much searching, I've found that the answer lies in understanding and living out our true identity in Christ. We live according to whom we think we are … or whom we believe we are. When you know the "why" to your life, the rest of the pieces of life fall into place. Our "why" is our identity. Yes, there have been countless books written on identity, but few go to the deepest part of our souls. This 40-day journey will show you the secret to unlocking and discovering your true identity. Identity is not impossible to find; identity is not a secret. It is an *invitation*. And it is open to anyone willing to take the journey of a lifetime.

Then, once you understand your true identity, purpose naturally follows. And this is why I wrote *Identity-Driven Purpose,* the book that goes along with this supplement, *A 40-Day Journey to Your New Identity in Christ*. Without knowing your identity, you will not know your purpose.

Know your identity, know your purpose. Live your life fulfilled and full of joy!

What is *identity* anyway?

Here are a few definitions:

- the fact of being who or what a person or thing is
- the distinguishing character or personality of an individual: *individuality*

The problem with these dictionary definitions of identity is the fact that they are vague. And when a person looks at identity from this viewpoint - individuality - they tend to become a person that someone else wants them to be. When it comes to identity, you cannot be unclear, and you cannot be tossed back and forth depending on what others say about you. If you are, you'll identify with the latest trend, your feelings, your peers, or perhaps something much more deceiving. Every person was created uniquely, designed with a distinct identity and purpose.

However, there are aspects of your identity that are shared by all of humanity. For example, everyone needs relationships. This is part of our identity. If you isolate yourself, for example, you will quickly find out that you are seeking out your identity in all the wrong places. So not only do you have a unique identity (think fingerprints), but you also have an element of your identity that is shared with others.

Simple, right? Just hang with me, and we will get to the bottom of everything.

Here is my definition of identity:

> *Your unique design and makeup that is meant to be shared with those around you.*

You were designed by Someone. Your makeup, your DNA, the very essence of who you are, is perfect. And all this package, all of who you are, is meant to be shared with those with whom you come into contact.

Also, your identity cannot change. Your *true* identity cannot change. The challenge that we are seeing today is that people are choosing their identity. Your identity cannot be chosen. It is not fluid. Yes, it can be influenced, but at the end of the day, your identity is ingrained so deeply into your DNA, that once it is fully discovered and allowed to flourish, peace, joy, purpose, and meaning in life simply pour out from this place.

The challenge with this topic is that people tend to think that if they change, then their identity changes. That is not true. Yes, people change. People are influenced. But deep inside your heart and your soul is a seed that has been waiting to be watered and nourished, so it can grow and flourish. My goal is to help you find the DNA of that seed, water it, and nourish it until the real you comes alive!

Let's get started!

How to use this book

*A 40-Day Journey to Your New Identity in Christ* is meant to be a supplement to your daily devotional time with God. If you are not currently reading the Bible every day, I encourage you to start there. Once you have done your daily Bible reading, then go to the appropriate day in this book and learn about what God has to say about you.

For 40 days, read one truth each day; do not try to tackle multiple days at a time. Take your time, relax, read the truths of scripture, and let them soak in.

The key to the success of this guide is not your commitment to finish but your commitment to *seek to understand*. Here is what I recommend. After you are finished reading each day's entry, stand in front of a mirror and review the scripture and the ensuing truth statement. Then look at yourself in the mirror and repeat the truth statement five times. Do this every day.

Why do this? Because repeating Biblical truths over yourself is a powerful way to encourage yourself with the truths of God. When you verbalize God's Word, the atmosphere around you changes. Your heart changes. Your soul changes. Everything changes. Best of all, you change!

All the truth statements can be found together in the back of the book, which makes it a bit easier to repeat them as you go through this study. Also, when I need a reminder of how God sees me and what He says about me, I simply turn to the back of this book and read the truth statements out loud. That easy exercise changes everything for me, and it can change your life too.

The scriptures found in this study are just the beginning of your identity in Christ. There are many more to be found in the Bible. Although this book lays a great foundation upon which you can build your life, it should never replace reading the Bible. Start reading the Bible every day.

Structurally, Days 1-19 are foundational truths about your identity. Then, Days 20-40 build upon this foundation. Like I mentioned above, take your time and do not rush through this. Every day really does build on the day before.

Also, you will see comments throughout this book about having said "yes" to Jesus. I repeat it many times because there may be people who read *A 40-Day Journey to Your New Identity in Christ* who have not accepted Jesus as their Savior, or perhaps there are people who have done so, but they really do not know what it means or if it was real.

Before moving on, I want to mention what the Bible says about salvation in Christ. The Bible does not tell us that we must pray a certain prayer or have our lives cleaned up before we can approach God. The Bible makes it very clear what needs to be done. This is found in Romans 10:8-13.

> "The word is near you, in your mouth and in your heart" (that is, the word of faith that we proclaim); because, if you confess with your mouth that Jesus is Lord and believe in your heart that God raised him from the dead, you will be saved. For with the heart one believes and is justified, and with the mouth one confesses and is saved. For the Scripture says, "Everyone who believes in him will not be put to shame." For there is no distinction between Jew and Greek; for the same Lord is Lord of all, bestowing his riches on all who call on

him. For "everyone who calls on the name of the Lord will be saved."

The Apostle Paul writes that we must believe with our heart, and we must confess with our mouth. Believe and confess what? Jesus is Lord over you and your life, and Jesus was raised from the dead and is seated in heaven at the right hand of God. There is not a certain prayer that you must pray, but you must simply confess, out loud, that Jesus was raised from the dead. Also, you must believe Jesus' words about himself: He was a real man, born of a virgin, who walked this earth and was God in the flesh. It is that simple. This is an *invitation*. Not from me, but from God Himself. If you have not confessed with your mouth that Jesus is your Lord and your Savior, then stop and do that right now.

Next, if you have not believed in your heart that God raised Jesus from the dead, but you are ready to believe that fact, then just say it out loud, as a confession. It could be something like this, "God, I believe that you raised Jesus from the dead."

Again, it is that simple.

At this point, you may have a lot of questions. First, I would recommend you get a Bible and start reading it. I always tell people to start with the book of John simply because it dives deeply into God's love for us, and we all need to know how much God loves us!

Next, if you are not part of a church, I would also recommend that you find a local church that you can start attending. Tell the pastor or someone at the church that you just accepted Jesus as your Lord and Savior and that you do truly believe that Jesus is Lord and that God raised Jesus from the dead. At that point, they will be able to help you learn more about Jesus. Lastly, I have prayed for you and will continue to pray for you. May God bless you as you embark on *A 40-Day Journey to Your New Identity in Christ!*

He opens before me the right path and leads me along in his footsteps of righteousness so that I can bring honor to his name.

Psalm 23:3
*The Passion Translation*

# A 40-Day Journey to Your New Identity in Christ

Day 1

John 1:12

But to all who did receive him, who believed in his name, he gave the right to become children of God.

Truth Statement:

I am a child of God.


*You are a child of God.* Let this truth sink in for a moment. If you have believed that Jesus is Lord and that God raised Jesus from the dead, He has given you the *right* to be a child of God. It is your right. You cannot earn it. The truth is this: *You are a child of God.*

The word "right" is the Greek word "*exousia.*" It means permission, physical and mental power, the power of authority, and the sign of regal authority, a crown.

Think about this for a moment. If you have received Jesus as your Lord and Savior and believed that God raised Him from the dead (Romans 10:9), Jesus has given you the *right*, the permission, the physical and mental power, the authority, and a *crown to wear* as a child of God! He has infused you with power and authority to stand before the Throne of Grace with confidence and authority, wearing your crown, and say confidently, "I am a child of God! I am your child, Lord! Father, Daddy, I am your son/daughter."

And Jesus looks at His Father and says, "Father, this is your child. Because of what I did, by dying on the cross and being raised to life at Your Right Hand, Father, I have given him/her the right to be your child."

Jesus looks at you with the most loving, compassionate eyes and beckons you to come near to Daddy.

Will you? Will you speak this truth over yourself? Close your eyes and picture the scene I described above. God does not care what your past is; He only cares about you. He loves you. He desires you. He has called you *child.*

This is your right. It has been given to you by Jesus. And nobody can take it away from you. Nobody. You are a child of God!

Day 2

John 15:1, 5

I am the true vine, and my Father is the vinedresser. I am the vine; you are the branches. Whoever abides in me and I in him, he it is that bears much fruit, for apart from me you can do nothing.

Truth Statement

I am a branch of the true vine and a channel of Christ's life.

To understand the truths of scripture, we must understand the context. When speaking these truths, Jesus was just about to be arrested and tortured for living a sinless, perfect life. He is pleading with His disciples - and with us - to abide in Him. Stay close to Him. Lean into Him. Obey Him. Remain in Him.

What does this mean? It means to not leave Him. Jesus is simply saying, "Stay with me. And when you stay with Me, we will work together to accomplish much for my Kingdom. You will bear much fruit."

Jesus is telling us to seek after Him and keep Him at the forefront of *everything* in our lives. And when we do that, He partners with us in *every aspect* of our lives.

In Psalm 16:8, King David uttered something amazing when he wrote, "I have set the Lord always before me; because He is at my right hand, I will not be shaken."

King David knew what it meant to abide in our Lord, to stay close to him. This sentence bears that out. David always put God before him in everything he did. By writing that God is at his right hand, David was declaring God's authority over every aspect of his life. I look at this statement with awe, and wonder to myself, "Can I do this?" So, I try. As much as I can remember to, I say, "God, I set you before me right now. May I see people the way you see people. And may I not bend to the demands of this world, but knowing you are always with me, I find rest and peace."

Now, do not hear something that is not here: *works*. Jesus is not saying that you need to do a lot of stuff for Him in order to be accepted. We just learned on Day 1 that we are a child of God and that the right was given to us. We did not earn the right. We did not deserve the right. Receiving what we did not earn or do not deserve is God's grace.

But Jesus does want us to be fruitful with our lives. We were put on this earth for a reason - to love God and to love others. Jesus is saying, "Walk with me always, and I will guide you all the days of your life and you will grow in love, joy, peace, patience, kindness, goodness, faithfulness, gentleness, and self-control" (Galatians 5:22-23).

When you do this, you are truly a conduit, a channel, for Christ to work through you, for His glory. Just like a pipe that delivers water to the root of a fruit tree, the power of Jesus flows to you and nourishes your roots, producing fruit in *every* season! The power of Jesus also flows *through* you to others, so that they, too, will produce fruit in their lives.

But, Jesus says, if you part ways with me, you will accomplish nothing for the Kingdom.

Do not leave Jesus' side. Walk with him. Talk with Him. Set Jesus always before you, at your right hand. Acknowledge Him and His ways every day!

Be a channel for the power, purpose, and identity of Christ today!

Day 3

John 15:15

No longer do I call you servants, for the servant does not know what his master is doing; but I have called you friends, for all that I have heard from my Father I have made known to you.

Truth Statement

I am a friend of Jesus.

This text is astonishing. It does not seem like much at first glance, but the implications are staggering. Why? Because Jesus said that He has made known to us what God has said. And while this was true when this text was written around 2,000 years ago, it is still true today. God, through His Holy Spirit still speaks to us today and makes known to us His will for our lives. He still speaks to us today. He is still our Friend.

Jesus, speaking to His disciples, and to us, has just laid out one of His commands. "Love one another," Jesus says, "as I have loved you. Greater love has no one than this, that someone lay down his life for his friends" (John 15:12-13).

Jesus has just told His disciples that He is their friend ... because He is about to lay down His life for them ... and for us! And He implores them - no, *commands* them - to love one another. The Greatest Commandment is *the* key to leading a meaningful, purposeful, and joyful life. And Jesus here is reminding us to love God and love others. This is our purpose in life.

But then Jesus takes it to another level. Jesus is saying that we are His friends. The Creator of the universe, the Word made flesh, is saying we are His friends. And why does He say this? Because Jesus makes known to us *everything* the Father has told Him.

Think for a moment about your best friend. You probably talk almost daily, and you typically will share things with that person that you do not share with others. You have a very intimate relationship where you can share anything with them and they still love you and accept you. It is like this with Jesus. You can talk to Him anytime, anywhere, and He is there for you, listening and not judging, guiding you through all the ups and downs of life.

12

Do not forget that Jesus actually fulfilled the prophecy above. He actually did lay His life down for you and for me.

Not only are you a friend of Jesus and not an enemy, but Jesus desires to make known *everything* He has heard from the Father. And what is more, He wants to reveal to us the deep things of the Father, the depths of our Father's heart. Abba, Daddy, wants to speak to us through His Holy Spirit. And Jesus has laid this out to us as a truth, *a promise.*

You are a friend of Jesus. Jesus left the earth which He said was better because He gave us the Holy Spirit and gave us our Advocate, Helper, the Spirit of Truth, who *dwells in us*. It is this love of Jesus as a friend of ours that is poured out into and through us via the Holy Spirit who reveals to us the deep things of our Father in Heaven (1 Corinthians 2:10).

Rejoice today! We are friends of Jesus! Walk with Him today. Talk to Him today. He is with you everywhere you go. Acknowledge your Friend's presence now and forever, and watch your life change!

Day 4

Romans 3:24

...[We] are justified by his grace as a gift, through the redemption that is in Christ Jesus...

Truth Statement

I am justified and redeemed.

You are justified, and you are redeemed! However, some of you might be asking the same question that I asked when I read this scripture, "What does that mean, to be justified and redeemed?"

I would guess that most of us understand what it means to be redeemed. When we think of redemption, we typically think of doing something better or making up for something that we did wrong or something that was done incorrectly. For example, in baseball you may hear, "Wow, the pitcher got himself into trouble by loading up the bases, but he redeemed himself by striking out the side."

But that is not the biblical definition of redeemed. The Greek word for redeemed is "*apolutrosis*," which means, "a releasing effected by the *payment of ransom*; liberation; deliverance."

This is the gospel! Jesus paid the ultimate price for you and me. He did this by releasing the grip of sin in our lives and, subsequently a life apart from God, and He made a way to God through His death, burial, and resurrection. Jesus made a payment for you. That payment, His death for our life, is the good news of Jesus! Jesus paid the ultimate, highest valued payment ever ... for YOU. Jesus gave up His life for you. What He did has far more worth and value than anything you can find here on earth because it has eternal implications. *Nothing* you attain on this earth will you take with you after death, except the transaction that Jesus paid and offers to you. Will you accept the liberation, the deliverance, the payment that Jesus paid? He is offering it. You just need to take it.

So, what does it mean to be justified? It means to "declare or pronounce someone to be just, righteous, or *as a person ought to be*." To be justified means that you have been pronounced by God as being in right standing with

Him. Not only that, but God continually looks upon you as one who is *as you ought to be:* justified despite your faults and failures.

This can seem complicated but let me try to simplify it. In this passage of scripture, the writer of Romans, the Apostle Paul, is saying that God sees us, *currently*, *right now, even in our brokenness and sin,* just as we ought to be, His Creation, His son or daughter. Not condemned, but *accepted.* And not only accepted but purchased with a price. God's only Son was the price paid for us! This is incredible!

Being justified and redeemed should lead us into a life of chasing after Jesus with everything we have and all that we are. Do we keep on sinning? By no means, says Paul in Romans 6:1! Understanding the price that has been paid and the way God sees us should break our sinful hearts and cause us to pursue God with all our heart, soul, mind, and strength!

If you are in Christ, meaning you have confessed with your mouth that Jesus is Lord and believed in your heart that God raised Him from the dead, then you *are* justified and redeemed before our Father in Heaven.

*IT IS DONE!* This means there is nothing you can do to earn this. It has already been paid, in full. The transaction is complete. You cannot pay anything or do anything to get it.

All you need to do is believe.

Day 5

Romans 6:6

We know that our old self was crucified with him [Jesus] in order that the body of sin might be brought to nothing, so that we would no longer be enslaved to sin.

Truth Statement

My old self was crucified with Christ, and I am no longer a slave to sin.

This is a powerful truth statement and a life-changing verse. Remember, the Bible is truth. It is up to us to believe it.

Let's break this down. "Our old self" means our former ways of life, our old, ancient, worn-out-by-use self. It also means our humanness, our human being, our nature. In other words, the way we were before believing in Jesus as our Savior. This old self has been crucified with Christ.

This is a huge concept that we must believe with our minds and with our hearts. Again, this is the truth. What the world teaches is not the truth. What the Bible says is true.

Paul is stating here in context that our faith, our belief in Jesus, has justified us and redeemed us. Refer back to Day 4 for more on this. This justification and redemption through Christ have come about because Jesus was crucified on our behalf. He became sin so that we are no longer judged by our sin. Instead, we are judged by what our relationship with Jesus is like. So, do we continue to sin? *God forbid,* is how Paul puts it! NO! Paul then writes that we have been crucified with Christ, buried with Christ, and raised with Christ in the newness of life! (We will study all of these in the coming days.) Paul explains that we have been planted together in the likeness of His death, and because of this, we are now to live in the likeness of His resurrection. Understanding the implications of His death and resurrection is key to living our lives from a place of *power.*

If we have Christ in us, if we believe and proclaim Jesus as Lord and that God raised Him from the dead, then we have died with Christ, and we have been raised with Him.

There is power in this confession. And that same power that raised Jesus from the grave is inside us because of the Holy Spirit that Jesus promised when He ascended into heaven.

You have the power not just to overcome sin, but you have the power that *has* overcome sin! That power is in you, and sin no longer has a grip on you. Your old self, pre-Christ, is dead. Your new self, your new person, is alive in Christ, and the power of sin in your life is OVER! DONE! But we must live every day reminding ourselves of this truth lest we fall back into the ways of this world and the sin that can entangle us.

But, you say, "I still sin." Yes, it happens. But if we focus on Jesus and not the sin, if we draw closer to the man Jesus and our Daddy in Heaven, sin will lose. Every time. This is how we are to live: free from the enslavement and entrapment of sin.

Today and every day, stay focused on Jesus and stop focusing on sin. Jesus is looking at you, and He is saying, "Look at me. *Look* at me. Draw near to me. Come to me. Your Daddy is here, right next to me, and He loves you. That sin life? It is dead to me. Focus on me, and watch it fade away."

Day 6

Romans 8:1

There is therefore now no condemnation for those who are in Christ Jesus.

Truth Statement

I am not and will not be condemned by God.

Let that truth statement soak in. *God does not and will not condemn you.* I know that for many of us, we grew up believing otherwise. We were taught that God is a mean, grumpy, old man sitting up in heaven looking down upon us with disappointment, just waiting for us to die and get to judgment day, so He can hammer us and then reluctantly "let us into heaven." *This is not true because this is not what the Bible says.*

Sadly, the chasm between the truth of the Bible and what the world and many well-meaning pastors, spiritual leaders, and priests teach can be vast.

It is important to understand what "condemnation" means. It means a damnatory or adverse sentence. We know that Jesus intercedes for us and presents us as righteous before God. And God agrees with His Son. If you have said "yes" to Jesus, you no longer have eternity apart from God to look forward to. Your eternity is secure with Him.

God loves you. He accepts you. And He does NOT condemn you. He sent His Son to this earth to be the payment and the ransom *so that* Daddy can have a loving relationship with us. He wants to be with us. He wants us to draw near to Him *so that* He can tell us how He sees us and how much He loves us.

Somehow there are teachings out there that want us to believe that God condemns us, that God is going to sentence us to damnation. For those of us in Christ, this is simply not true! Will there be a judgment day? Absolutely. The Bible teaches this. But the judgment day is not a day of condemnation. It is an actual time that God has appointed for you. And it is a moment of celebration! Why? Because it is the final step before we enter into glory with Him in heaven.

For the "dead," those who have not received Jesus and proclaimed Him as

Lord and Savior and believed that God raised Him from the dead, that day will be a terrible day. Yes, on that day, they will enter into eternity separated, apart from God.

But for us who do confess Christ, we will be judged by what we did with our lives after we accepted Christ. This is not an invitation to works, to earn favor. Remember, Christ already paid the price for you. Jesus is the Judge (John 5:22), and He loves you so much that He died for you. Think about this. Is He going to condemn you after dying for you? No. Rest assured that Jesus does not condemn you, nor does our Daddy in Heaven.

Go today in the assurance that God does not condemn you. He loves you.

Day 7

<u>Romans 15:13</u>

May the God of hope fill you with all joy and peace in believing, so that by the power of the Holy Spirit you may abound in hope.

<u>Truth Statement</u>

I am filled with joy and peace, and I abound in hope.

Do you believe it? Do you believe that you are filled with joy and peace, and that you abound in hope? Many people today are leading lives so filled with anxiety and stress that the concept of being filled with joy, peace, and abounding in hope seems impossible. Today I have good news. It is not only possible, but it is also already within you.

Today's verse starts with a fact: God is hope. The writer of the book of Romans, the Apostle Paul, is saying that God is the author of hope. Hope is God's idea. He created it, and He has filled you with it.

Yahweh, the God of hope, desires to fill you with all joy and peace in believing. Let's break this down. You might notice the word "may" being used twice in this sentence. That word does not exist in the Greek or Arabic translations. When Paul wrote this sentence, he was more accurately writing it as a promise, a present-tense fact, something that has already taken place. This part of the sentence should read, "The God of hope fills you with all joy in believing," to help us understand this is a promise that *has been fulfilled*. God has already done it!

A more precise translation of the word "believing" is the word *trust*. Therefore, what Paul has written here could be stated as follows: *As you trust in God, the God of hope, He will fill you with joy and peace.*

The word joy could also be translated as the word *gladness* or even *rejoicing*. However, even these words do not fully describe what Paul is trying to express. This joy, gladness, or rejoicing needs to have a few descriptors added to it, such as *exceeding, the fullness of,* and *overflowing*. One of the reasons there are so many different translations of the Bible is because it is very difficult to translate from Hebrew, Greek, and Arabic into English in a succinct, effective, and accurate way.

The word peace means tranquility and safety. It is God's desire that we be filled with gladness, tranquility, and safety! We will dive deeper into the full meaning of the word *peace* on day 34 of this study.

Finally, for today, Paul writes that we are to abound in hope. How? Through the power of the Holy Spirit. In other words, the Holy Spirit in you can empower you into hope. But not just hope, *abounding* hope. Let's break this one down a bit further.

The word *abound* is the Greek word *"perisseuo."* This is a verb, an action word, one that implies that it is currently happening or has the capacity to happen at any moment. *Perisseuo* means "to exceed a fixed number of measure" and is often used for describing a flower going from a bud to full bloom. Implied in this text is not just to overflow and exceed what is perceived as a fixed measure or amount. Paul desires that the hope that is in us through the Holy Spirit causes us to be seen by others *coming alive with hope,* that the people around us would see us in full bloom with joy! Amazing!

Let's rewrite this sentence based on what we have just learned:

*As you trust more and more in the God of hope, through His Spirit, the Holy Spirit, the exceedingly overflowing fullness of joy, and an overwhelming peace, tranquility, and safety will flow into and through you causing you to confidently come alive and blossom with hope, anticipation, and expectation in a way that others look upon as beautiful.*

Today, trust in God and see how His Holy Spirit creates breakthrough in and through you in a way you could never have imagined!

Day 8

<u>Romans 8:17</u>

And if children, then heirs - heirs of God and fellow heirs with Christ, provided we suffer with him in order that we may also be glorified with him.

<u>Truth Statement</u>

As a child of God, I am a fellow heir with Christ.


So far in our journey together, we have established that you are a child of God. We started this 40-day journey with that truth on Day 1. So, when Paul writes, "...and if children," he is referring again to those who are in Christ. If you have not believed in Jesus Christ as Savior, then this does not apply to you. But for those who have, you are an heir of God and a fellow heir with Christ.

This...is...good...news! This is the love of Daddy and Jesus for you!

As a child of God, you are an heir of God and a fellow heir with Christ. This means that God has given you an inheritance, the same inheritance He gave to Jesus, and Jesus shares it with you. (See Hebrews 2:11; Romans 8:29; Mark 3:34, for more on Jesus as our Brother.)

The Greek for an heir is "*kleronomos*." It means one who receives by lot and heir, *one who receives his allotted possession by right of sonship,* and one who *has obtained* the portion allotted to him.

Whew! This is huge. Let's go deeper.

As an heir, you are a son or daughter. Jesus is the firstborn; He is the Son. But Daddy and Jesus are sharing that with you. You are a son or a daughter. You have received this because of what Jesus did. And read the words carefully … it is a *right* that you have. Again, if needed, go back to Day 1. God has given you the right to be a son or daughter, and Jesus is sharing this right with you. This is LOVE!

What is the "portion" allotted to you? It is the inheritance. Because you are a son or daughter, you receive the inheritance, the fullness of Christ in you. This means everything that Jesus has you have. Right now. At this moment. It is yours! We just need to believe it and receive it into our lives. As you study the Bible, and as you continue in this study, God will reveal more about His inheritance to you.

Finally, the verse goes on to say, "provided that we suffer with him." Here is the bottom line: If you have accepted Christ, you will have troubles. But let me ask you this: Are you not already having trouble in this life? Is that not one of the reasons that we are on this journey together? One of the outcomes of our time together is to learn how to overcome these troubles through Christ.

And, while we will not go deep on the topic of suffering in this study, take heart, because Jesus says, "I have overcome the world" (John 16:33)!

Trust Him today. You are an heir of God and a fellow heir of Jesus!

Day 9

<u>Romans 15:7</u>

Therefore welcome one another as Christ has welcomed you, for the glory of God.

<u>Truth Statement</u>

I am accepted by Christ.


What does welcoming someone have to do with being accepted by Christ? This is part of the challenge with the English language. It does not always translate the words from their original meanings well. The word "welcome" here is the Greek word *"proslambano"* which means to take as one's companion, to take by the hand in order to lead, *to grant access to one's heart.*

The last part of that definition is closer to the original meaning of the word. *To grant access to one's heart.* Let's use this phrase as a replacement for the word "welcome" and see how it reads.

*Therefore, grant access to one another's hearts as Christ has granted you access to His heart, for the glory of God.*

This makes all the difference. Jesus has already granted you access to His heart. Everything He has is yours, including His heart. Draw near to Him, and He will draw near to you. He wants to tell you what He thinks of you, how He feels about you, how He died for you, and what that does to *His* heart. Seriously. This is the truth (See Ephesians 1:12).

In the same way that Jesus has granted us access to His heart, we are to do the same for others. One of the main points of my book, *Identity-Driven Purpose,* is that we are to fulfill the Great Commandment through our purpose in life, which is loving God and others. We are to open up our hearts to others because this glorifies God.

Now, a word of caution here. You also need to guard your heart, because from the heart flows the wellspring of life (Proverbs 24:3). We are not to give our hearts to those who hurt us, nor throw pearls to swine. We have the mind of Christ, remember? That means we are discerning, and we have wisdom. "As innocent as a dove but as wise as a serpent" is how Jesus said we should be (Matthew 10:16). Be wise, be smart. Do not give your heart to someone who is going to trample on it. But do give your heart to those you can trust, because this is glorifying to God. Why? God desires unity in his Church, His Bride. It glorifies God when we are unified because it is then "that the world may know that Jesus is the Son of God" (John 17:23).

Today, know that you are accepted by Jesus because He has opened up His heart to you and has invited you into that deep place of love with Him. Now, give your heart to Him.

Day 10

1 Corinthians 1:30

And because of him you are in Christ Jesus, who became to us wisdom from God, righteousness and sanctification and redemption.

Truth Statement

In Christ Jesus, I have wisdom, righteousness, sanctification, and redemption.

It is Day 10, and your world is about to get rocked again! If you have believed in Christ, He has given you wisdom, righteousness, sanctification, and redemption. *He has given it to you.* Will you take it? It truly is yours for the taking, but you need to grasp it and take hold of it.

This verse speaks of God, and the amazing things He has done for us through His Son, Jesus. It is because of God, the verse says, that we are in Christ Jesus. Being "in Christ" is our position in life. We have Christ in us because He is in us via the Holy Spirit. And because we are in Christ, Jesus has become to us wisdom, righteousness, sanctification, and redemption. Let's break these down.

We get the English word *wisdom* from the Greek word "*sophia*." It means to be broad and full of intelligence, knowing very diverse matters, able to learn, the ability to discover the meaning of mysteries, skill in the management of affairs, the ability to talk to people about Christ, and the knowledge and ability to live a godly and upright life. *This word, sophia, describes you!* Again, you have wisdom. Grasp it and take hold of it!

The Greek word "*dikaiosune*" is where we get the English word *righteousness*. This is similar to Day 4's word *justified*. It means that you are as you ought to be. God sees you exactly as you ought to be. Complete. Whole. Filled with wisdom and able to accomplish much in your life for the Kingdom. It also means acceptable to God. Because of Jesus, you are acceptable to God. Remember, God is perfect. He is the true manifestation of that righteousness and more. God is perfect and perfectly holy, sinless, and awesome. In our state before accepting Christ, we would stand before God and be judged as guilty. But because of Christ, we now stand before

26

God, boldly and courageously, as acceptable and accepted.

The Greek word *"hagiasmos"* is translated into the English word *sanctification*. It simply means that because of Jesus, we are purified and consecrated. In other words, we are presented as holy and pure before God *because of what Jesus did for us.* We ARE purified and consecrated before God. There is nothing we need to do to become more purified and consecrated. God sees us this way because of what Jesus accomplished on the cross.

The Greek word *"apolutrosis"* is translated into the English word *redemption.* We covered this on Day 4. If needed, go and review Day 4 again for more on what it means to be redeemed. It is repeated here for good reason. Understanding what redemption means in your life and that you *are* redeemed is a major concept that needs to be completely understood in order to live a restored life, fully alive for God.

In Christ, as ones who have said "yes" to Jesus, we *have* wisdom, righteousness, sanctification, and redemption. It is ours. We cannot earn it, we cannot pay for it, we cannot do anything for it. We can only receive it. It is being offered to you right now. Take it. It is yours.

Day 11

1 Corinthians 6:19-20

Do you not know that your body is a temple of the Holy Spirit within you, whom you have from God? You are not your own; you were bought with a price.

Truth Statement

My body is a temple of the Holy Spirit who dwells in me.

Day 11 picks up where Day 10 left off. Today's verse ends with, "...you were bought with a price." As a reminder, you are redeemed because Jesus paid a hefty price - His life - for you. Because of this, we are not our own; we belong to Jesus.

But this is GOOD NEWS! Some may be saying, "I do not want to belong to anyone." I understand that thought, but as a love-response to Jesus for what He did, not being our own should be a natural outflow of love back to Him. We love God because He first loved us. It is not out of duty, but out of love by realizing the gravity of the price He paid. No guilt-love. No obligation-love. Love-love. Loving God because He first loved us. Loving God because we understand how He sees us and what He thinks about us and what He has done for us.

If this is difficult to understand, ask the Holy Spirit for help. If you are in Christ - if you have confessed with your mouth that Jesus is Lord and believed in your heart that God raised Jesus from the dead - you are saved and in Christ. And because you are in Christ, you have the Holy Spirit in you. In the Bible, the Holy Spirit is called Counselor, Comforter, and Advocate. The Holy Spirit also encompasses all wisdom. The fullness of the Holy Spirit, all of the Holy Spirit, all of His attributes, are living *in you right now.*

And your body is the temple of the Holy Spirit. A temple is a place of worship, the dwelling place of God. Again, stop and think about this: The Holy Spirit, the One whom Jesus said would come, dwells within you. Because we have the Holy Spirit dwelling within us, God has cleansed us to a point that He is pleased to have the Holy Spirit dwell with us, among us, within us. Incredible!

This should compel us to love. God has made a deposit into our bodies guaranteeing the inheritance promised to us.

But that is not all. The Holy Spirit in us is waiting for us to ask and *activate* Him on our behalf. In my book, *Identity-Driven Purpose,* I reference several other resources that explain who the Holy Spirit is much better than I can. The Holy Spirit is a Gentleman, and He will not unwillingly interfere. But, when asked to help, He shows up, every time. Try it. Say, "Holy Spirit, I give you permission to rise up in me today. Holy Spirit, help me understand scripture. Holy Spirit, help me to love today. Holy Spirit, help me be a better husband/wife today. Holy Spirit, help me be a better dad/mom today." He will help. Every time.

Day 12

Ephesians 1:13

In him you also, when you heard the word of truth, the gospel of your salvation, and believed in him, were sealed with the promised Holy Spirit...

Truth Statement

I am sealed with the Holy Spirit that was promised to me.

My prayer for you today is to understand the promised gift that God has given to you. This gift - the gift of His Spirit, the Holy Spirit - is the best of all the spiritual gifts and truly gives you an unfair advantage in life while living in this world.

Take note of the word "sealed" in this verse. It is a very important and powerful word. This is the Greek word *"sphragizo,"* which means, "to set a seal upon, to mark with a seal." But that's not all.

*Sphragizo,* or "to seal" also means to be sealed for security from Satan. This lines up with the scripture where the Apostle John writes in 1 John 5:18 that Satan cannot touch us. Really? I thought that the thief (Satan) comes to steal, kill, and destroy? And that if we resist the devil, he will flee from us, which implies that the devil can influence us somehow?

This is all true, but there is something in the deeper meaning of this verse that we must understand. Jesus promised the Holy Spirit to us. In fact, Jesus said it was better that He leave this earth so that the Holy Spirit would come. See John 16:7.

Quick review - when you said "yes" to Jesus, you were immediately filled with the Holy Spirit. That is the promise referred to in this passage of scripture. You are filled with the Holy Spirit. The Holy Spirit resides in you, lives in you. Always. He is always with you. He never leaves you and will never forsake or abandon you (Matthew 28:20).

However, you must allow the Holy Spirit to work in your life. The Holy Spirit has been referred to as a Gentleman. He will not barge His way into your life and force you to do things or force God's will upon your life. However, if you ask Him, acknowledge Him, and allow Him full reign of

30

your heart and mind, He will awaken within you. And, according to this verse, the Holy Spirit will hide you from Satan. You are literally hidden from Satan.

But there's a caveat here, a step that we *must take* for this seal to work properly. We must ask the Holy Spirit to hide us from the works of the enemy.

Because we can talk to God, and He hears us (1 John 5:14), we should talk to Him. It is that simple. God wants to talk to you via His Holy Spirit. But we must make the first move (James 4:8).

Right now, first thank God for giving you His Spirit, and for His Spirit being in you. Then ask the Holy Spirit to come alive in you today - *right now!* Ask to *be filled* with the Holy Spirit, right now. Ask the Holy Spirit to lead you into all truth and to guide you through your day, and *every day.* And ask the Holy Spirit to protect you from our adversary, the devil.

Finally, what was this "unfair advantage" that I referred to earlier? It is simply this: When you go into the world today, there are many people who do not have the Holy Spirit. But you do. Ask the Holy Spirit to guide you when you have troubles, problems, or want to knowingly sin. Ask Him to lead you into all wisdom and truth. He will. The Bible says that the Holy Spirit searches the "deep things" of our Father in Heaven (1 Corinthians 2:10). Imagine that! These "deep things" are the *depths, the mysteries* of God. WOW! God reveals His mysteries to us via the Holy Spirit. This gives us a *tremendous advantage in life!*

This revelation is the greatest spiritual gift that God has given us through His Son, Jesus. Embrace and allow the Holy Spirit to lead you in every way today - and every day!

Day 13

1 Corinthians 6:17

But he who is joined to the Lord becomes one spirit with him.

Truth Statement

I am joined to the Lord and am one spirit with Him.


OK, this is a huge topic and one that is not easily understood. But again, this is truth, this is reality. God is One (Deuteronomy 6:4). He is all-knowing, ever-present, and everywhere. God is also Spirit (John 4:24). The Spirit of God is what Jesus gave to you when you said "yes" to Him. Jesus is also God (John 1:1, 14). He was fully man and fully God while on earth (Colossians 2:9). Again, this is a difficult concept to grasp, but instead of trying to rationalize it, just believe it. In the book of Genesis, it talks about God, Jesus, and the Holy Spirit all being together at the beginning of the creation of the universe. We see this throughout scripture, too. This is what makes Jesus' life and death so compelling: He left the "comfort" of his relationship with Father in Heaven to come to earth, totally and completely submitted to Daddy, to Father, and lived a *perfect* life. Then He died. Voluntarily. For you. For me. He did this so that we can be one with Daddy, Jesus, and Spirit as well. He died so that we can be made perfect (Hebrews 10:14). And those of us who have said "yes" to Jesus *are being* sanctified (which simply implies that we are walking with Jesus).

With that basic understanding, the reality is that when we say "yes" to Jesus, we are joined with Him and are one spirit with Him. This means that Jesus pours out, or releases His authority through the Holy Spirit in our lives. Since we are all made in the image of God, we have the Holy Spirit with us or at least the ability for the Spirit of God to activate our spirit man, the inmost aspect of ourselves. This spirit in us is what the Bible many times calls the "heart" (Romans 5:5 and Ephesians 3:17). The reality is that the Holy Spirit is in us, and the Holy Spirit is God. So, when we say "yes" to Jesus, we become one with Jesus, one spirit with God.

And do you want more Good News? The Bible says, "For the Spirit searches everything, even the depths of God" (1 Corinthians 2:10). This means that we can connect to, be led by, and hear from God Himself through the Holy

Spirit! This is where we find the ability to understand our identity and our ultimate purpose in life - to love God and love others. AND the Holy Spirit gives us the ability, the strength, the sight, and the direction to fulfill this in our lives and in the lives of those we encounter.

Being joined to the Lord and being one spirit with Him is an amazing reality. And once you understand and experience this reality, your life will be forever changed.

Day 14

2 Corinthians 2:14

But thanks be to God who always leads us in triumphal procession in Christ and who makes known through us the fragrance that consists of the knowledge of him in every place.

Truth Statement

God leads me in triumph with Christ and in the knowledge of Christ.

Day 14 is special. Get ready. Hang on. God leads us in triumphal procession in Christ!

When you think of a procession, you probably think of a parade. Now, think of a parade that is being led by God, and we are following Him with Jesus next to us. What are we celebrating or being led in a celebration, or a grandiose show, toward? Eternity with God. We triumph with God through Christ over death. There is no permanent death for us, only eternity with God. The word picture that Paul is painting here is that, like Paul, we are led *by God Himself* to our ultimate death *in triumph over death.* Yes, we will die, and this physical body as we know it will cease to function. But our souls remain and are joined with God in heaven. God always leads us in our lives to death over this world and everything in it toward eternity with Him. The goal in this procession is to live our lives as "dead" to this world and "alive" through Christ. Like the writer of Hebrews mentions, we have no more fear of death. And when that fear is gone, we can truly live, fearlessly.

I will stop here because this is a much larger discussion that goes very, very deep. Pause. Reflect on what you just read.

The passage goes on to say that Jesus makes known, through us, *the fragrance of the knowledge of Him in every place*. Again, Paul is referring to himself here, but he is also referring to all Christians as to how we should live. Everywhere we go Christ makes known - not us, but Jesus - the fragrance of the knowledge of Him. Through us, Christ *uses* us to make Himself known to people. A fragrance is a pleasant smell that is given off of something. In this picture, that fragrance is given off by us *for God.* Our lives are to be a pleasant fragrance to God through Christ in us by the way we impact the Kingdom.

*The knowledge of Him in every place* refers to the fact that this fragrance is based on our knowledge of Christ and what we do with Him in our lives. Do we share? Do we talk about Him? Do we lead a life worthy of His death?

The point we need to understand today is that, if we let Him, God will lead us in our lives. And as He leads us, we have victory over everything in this life *if* we are led by Christ and the Holy Spirit. Remember, the Holy Spirit searches the deep things of our Father in Heaven, so our knowledge of Jesus should be growing more and more as we grow older and grow in our knowledge of Him. Hebrews talks of not drinking milk anymore but rather eating solid food (Hebrews 5:13-14). This means we are to grow up (or be a grown up, to be an adult) in Christ and grow deeper in our understanding of who He is and what He did for us.

Today, know that you are being led in triumph over death and that God wants to reveal more and more of who He is and who His Son is to you *and through you to others*. Pray for the Holy Spirit to reveal to you the characteristics of His Son, Jesus.

Day 15

2 Corinthians 3:14

But their minds were closed. For to this very day, the same veil remains when they hear the old covenant. It has not been removed because only in Christ is it taken away.

Truth Statement

The hardening of my mind and the veiling of my eyes have been removed in Christ.

This very interesting passage is also discussed in the book of Hebrews, and the overarching message is this: A veil has been removed from your eyes and mind.

What is a veil? In this context, Paul is writing about the veil that Moses put on after he met with God because his face was radiant from the powerful encounter with God. This story is found in Exodus 34:29-35. A veil is essentially a piece of fabric that blocks our view and keeps us from understanding. For us today, this is not a piece of fabric but rather a mindset of disbelief. Because of Jesus, we now have the ability to understand and comprehend the things of God.

You have the mind of Christ now that you have said "yes" to Him. Because of this, the truth of the Bible can now fill your mind and heart, and the Holy Spirit is with you waiting for you to ask for help with understanding.

If you recall yesterday's message about the knowledge of Christ being a fragrance through us in our lives as we turn from this world and turn to Jesus, this is made possible because the veil that has been over our eyes and minds *has been removed*. God now wants you to go deeper than ever into the mysteries of the Kingdom. These mysteries are found in the Bible, and they are available to you. Just ask, read, and pray.

Another point in this passage is that there are still many people out there with a hardened mind and a veil over their eyes. They simply cannot understand the truths of the Bible, especially the truths of Jesus Christ. It is interesting because many people will read the Bible and say it is a great book and admit that it might even have some historical truths to it. But when it comes to

Jesus, the Son of God, and all that He did and accomplished - and especially that He was raised from the dead and ascended into heaven - THAT is a fact that some people just cannot believe. By accepting Jesus and opening up the door for the Holy Spirit to reveal truths to you, a more thorough and truthful understanding of this reality, that Jesus was resurrected and sits with our Father in Heaven, will begin to unfold in your mind and your heart.

Today, remind yourself that your mind is open to the truths of the Bible, and your eyes will begin to see the deep truths of the Kingdom of God. There is *nothing* more exciting and just plain awesome than understanding the keys to the Kingdom. Celebrate! You have the mind of Christ!

Day 16

2 Corinthians 5:17

So then, if anyone is in Christ, he is a new creation; what is old has passed away - look, what is new has come!

Truth Statement

I am a new creature in Christ.

Welcome to your new life! I write this because it is true - if you are in Christ. Once you say "yes" to Jesus, you are a new creation. Gone is the old way of life. Here to stay is the new way and the new life.

Sounds good, right? It is not quite as simple as it sounds, however. Yes, the truth is that you are a new creation in Christ. The challenge lies in our believing this truth. This is why I wrote *Identity-Driven Purpose*: to help you understand your identity and purpose in life, which includes living your life from the understanding that you *are a new creation*. However, the reality is that *it is just not that easy to do*.

We have to take hold of this truth, that we are new creatures in Christ, and *live every day in light of this truth*. I write about it in depth in my book, but the reality is that this is a mindset change, a focus on things not of this world but on things "above" where Christ is seated. We must be constantly mindful that we are new creatures in Christ.

You see, Jesus died and three days later was resurrected by the same power that now resides in us (Romans 8:11). This power that is in us is what allows us to see, believe, and live a life as a new creature in Christ. The main challenge in all of this lies in this question: Do you *want* to live a new life in Christ?

Today, if you say "yes" to this question, that you DO want to live a new life in Christ, then get up, right now, go to the mirror, and do the exercise.

If you need to, review the introduction as a reminder of how to perform the daily exercise of speaking the truth of God over your life.

There is power in your spoken words.

Speak this truth over yourself today.

Allow the truth of scripture to wash over you and watch how the Power of the Holy Spirit moves in your life!

Your new life in Christ begins right now!

Day 17

2 Corinthians 5:21

God made the one who did not know sin to be sin for us, so that in him we would become the righteousness of God.

Truth Statement

I have become the righteousness of God in Christ.

Follow the logic of this statement from the Apostle Paul in his letter to the Corinthians (and us):

- "God made the one that did not know sin…" This is Jesus.
- "…to be sin for us…" When Jesus died, he took on our sin, my sin, your sin, and paid the final price - the sacrifice of His life - for our sins.
- "…so that in him…" In Him also means through Him. You are in Him if you have said "yes" to Jesus.
- "…we would become the righteousness of God." God sees us as righteous because of Jesus' sacrifice.

This … is … a … big … deal! You must get this and understand it in order to fully live in the reality of your new identity in Christ.

Jesus lived a sinless life. Perfection. Total and complete perfection here on earth. Because of this, Jesus became the spotless sacrifice, the "spotless lamb" (1 Peter 1:19), *perfection* for our *imperfection.* We must understand and confess to God that we have sinned and fallen short of God's glory (Romans 3:23). Do not focus on the concept of sin right now; it just means you have missed the mark in God's plan for your life. Sin manifests in many forms, but just know every single human being that has ever walked this earth has sinned - and does sin - except Jesus Christ.

Because Jesus lived a perfect life, He died an unjust and horrific death in place of you and me. He did this for everyone. *Everyone.* You see, before Jesus came onto the scene, in order to have your sins forgiven, the Jews would appoint a priest to make a sacrifice of an animal on behalf of the Jewish people. They called this a sacrifice for all their "accidental" sins. The problem, as explained in the book of Hebrews, is that the priest himself was also imperfect, and therefore he had to make a sacrifice for himself also. This all took place in the temple, next to the Holy of Holies, the Ark of the Covenant, the location in Jerusalem where the Presence of God literally dwelled.

Along came Jesus, the Answer to over 300 Old Testament prophecies, and because He lived a perfect life, He became that sacrifice for the Jews - *and for us* (Romans 1:16). Jesus died for me and you so that we can have access - direct access - to the Creator of the Universe and the Creator of everything that was and is created. Why is this important to understand? Because without Jesus and His sacrifice, death, and resurrection, in the presence of God, we could not stand or appear. God embodies absolute perfection, and without Jesus, even our souls could not be in His presence. That is how perfect God is and how imperfect we are.

*But* ... because of Jesus and His sacrifice, we now have access to our Perfect Father in Heaven, through Jesus. Remember, Jesus is seated, right now, at the right hand of the Father - right next to Him.

But get this, we are now the righteousness of God because of this sacrifice of Jesus. Some of you are saying right now, "I do not get it." It took me a while to get it as well. Let me go deeper. What Paul is essentially saying is that because of what Jesus did, God looks at us as righteous, as "having been made right" in our standing with God. Again, this is a big deal because remember, we cannot stand before God and live. But because of Jesus, we now can. So now, we have access to our Father in Heaven, and we can approach Him about anything.

Let me repeat - This ... is ... a ... big ... deal.

So, pray for understanding if you still do not fully understand. The Holy Spirit will reveal the truth to you if you ask Him.

41

Day 18

Galatians 3:28

There is neither Jew nor Greek, there is neither slave nor free, there is neither male nor female, for you are all one in Christ Jesus.

Truth Statement

I have been made one with all who are in Christ Jesus.

Inclusion. Is this not something we all desire in our hearts, to be included? How many of us have been the last one chosen for the pick-up baseball team as a kid? I have. And I hated it. It is interesting, this concept of being excluded from something. What is it that causes fear to well up whenever there is a gathering, a party, a celebration in which we are not included? In today's context, it is most likely to occur online in a social networking context. It is the feeling of being left out, the fear of not being included, or of missing out (FOMO). It has happened to all of us, and it is not a good feeling at all.

The reality in our lives, however, if we are willing to accept it, is that we have been included in something far greater than our minds can at most times comprehend. It is called the Kingdom of God. And it is something of which we are a part if we have said "yes" to Jesus.

In this Kingdom, which is ruled and reigned over by a loving King, the Bible says there is no Jew or Greek. What does this mean? Paul is saying there is no difference between people no matter their background as long as they have said "yes" to Jesus. Now, this was downright scandalous in Jesus' day. So much so, it cost Jesus His life. Yes, Jesus came for the Jews, to return them to their First Love. But He also came for everyone, for me, for you. And He does not care what your religious background is, even if there is no religious background at all. If that describes you, one of no religious background, you probably are in a better position of understanding the truths of the Kingdom of God than those with religious backgrounds. Clearing the mind and the heart of years and years of rule-following and ceremonial obedience can cost someone their personal relationship with Jesus Christ. Paul is saying that no matter your background, you are equal in the Kingdom of God.

In the Kingdom of God, there is neither slave nor free. What? I thought it was for freedom that Jesus set us free? And why does Paul talk about slavery? The slavery Paul is referring to is two-fold: the spiritual slave and the bondservant slave. Slavery, in Paul's day, was common, as were those who were free. Paul is simply saying that in God's Kingdom, we are all one with Him. We are all equal.

In the Kingdom of God, there is neither male nor female. Paul is stating that, in God's Kingdom, Jesus sees everyone the same and accepts everyone equally.

Paul's true words about the Kingdom are hard for some to accept. In God's eyes, if you have said "yes" to His Son Jesus, you are family, you are an heir, you are a son or daughter, and you are one of Abraham's offspring. This was a hard saying for the Jews of that day and for the Jews of today. This is a hard saying today for *anyone* who sees others as less than, or otherwise inferior. Those who see others through the lens of inferiority have an anti-Kingdom mindset and will not be free even in the Kingdom of God.

Today, you are equal, accepted, included, loved, and an heir to the King of kings. And if you have said "yes" to Jesus, nobody can take that away from you. Nobody. Rejoice today as a family member in the Kingdom of God!

Day 19

Galatians 4:7

So you are no longer a slave but a son, and if you are a son, then you are also an heir through God.

Truth Statement

As an heir of God, I am free from the traps of this world.


As a son or a daughter in God's Kindom here on earth, I do not have to live my life as a slave. The mindset that we should have as sons and daughters is one of freedom. No matter what my circumstances, if I hold on to the fact that I am a son and not a slave, I can acutally live a life of freedom no matter what this life may throw at me.

As many of you have experienced, this world is full of traps, pitfalls, dangers, some of which are under our control and some others which are not. As a son or daughter in God's Kingdom, there is freedom from all of the entrapments of this world because you have a Guide who wants to lead you to freedom. It is this freedom that God offers, a freedom unlike any other found on earth, that Paul is referring to in today's verse when he says that we are no longer a slave but a *son or daughter*. And because we are a son or daughter, we are an heir of Jesus through God. Some of you may be saying something like, "So what?" or "I do not get it." Let me explain.

Paul is explaining that all of us, at one point in our lives (and currently for some of us), have been enslaved to the elementary principles of this world. Another translation is "elemental spirits." Whichever translation you read, it is still a true statement. The principles of this world, the powers of this world, the rulers and authorities of this world, the false teachings of this world, have created for us entrapments and enslavement. Many in North America are blind to this reality, as we will see on Day 20. For others, this *is* their reality. Just take a look at China for example. Behind North Korea, it is the most brutal, dishonest, controlling, corrupt, and insidious regime on the planet. Millions, or perhaps billions, are enslaved to their government's power and control. These people are enslaved. But there are millions, perhaps billions, in China that are not enslaved, yet they live under the control of this terrible governmental regime. What am I talking about?

44

I am referring to the underground church in China. Under the iron fist of Xi Jingping and his henchmen are perhaps billions of free people in Christ, living a life of total freedom in Jesus while fully under the "rule" of Xi. How is this possible?

The reality is this is happening in the United States, too. There are basic and elementary principles in this world that try to rule, control, and pervert the reality of the Kingdom of God. But for those who have their eyes and their minds opened, the reality of the Kingdom has transformed their heart, and because of this, they are free and are sons and daughters. You see, Paul is referring to the fact that Jesus came to redeem those who were under the Jewish law and control, but Paul's statement here transcends time and refers to other controlling groups as well. And Jesus came to redeem those who are under those laws to be adopted into the Kingdom. And because we say "yes" to Jesus, we say "yes" to Father, to Daddy. And this makes us sons and daughters and heirs to the King of kings.

Rejoice today knowing you are an heir in the Kingdom of God and that the traps of this world no longer have a hold on you!

Day 20

Galatians 5:1

For freedom Christ has set us free.

Truth Statement

I have been set free in Christ.

Today we continue the idea of freedom. However, in today's study, we focus on the choices we make in life that can cause us to be in bondage.

Remember, Christ has come to set us free. It is for freedom that Christ set us free. It seems redundant, but that is great news! Jesus came to release you as a captive to the ways of this world. In this verse, Paul is referring to the Jewish law that said that you had to be circumcised as an adult (ouch!) in order to be a Jew. Some early Christians were giving in to the pressure they were receiving from Jewish leaders that they had to be circumcised even though they had given their lives over to Jesus. Paul is pleading with his readers not to follow through with it, because if they do, then Christ is of no use to them. Why? Because they would have given in to the ways of the world and not to the ways of Christ.

Let's put that into today's context. Say you accepted Jesus as a child, and you have been living a good life. You follow the rules nicely, attend church every week, read the Bible a few times a year, and generally lead a safe life. In reality, this is a life of slavery. This is not freedom. You see, you have fallen victim to the rules of Christianity, that to be a good person, you have to do a bunch of stuff so that God will like you, accept you, and so that you look good to everyone around you. This is called "wearing the mask."

Paul is saying that Jesus came so that we do not have to follow a set of rules, but rather we follow - and fall in love with - the man Jesus, and walk day-by-day in His love and leading through the Holy Spirit.

Let me give you another example. Let's say you have been a Christian for ten years, but you are still looking at porn. You are a slave. Or, let me use a less extreme and more acceptable example. Let's say you overeat or drink too much. How much is too much? You know. The Spirit speaks to us.

Whichever desires of the flesh you are gratifying, these are causing slavery in your life. You are in bondage to that behavior. Jesus is calling us to a life of freedom where food, anger, control, people-pleasing, sexual addictions, or any addiction for that matter, no longer control us. Jesus is calling us to a life where we are no longer controlled by that behavior. We are now free!

Today, say "yes" again to Jesus and start fresh. Tell yourself that you are no longer a slave and that you have been set free in Jesus Christ and start living that out today. Right now. Remember, you have the Holy Spirit in you, and you have the mind of Christ. You can say no to the things that control you.

Day 21

Ephesians 1:3

Blessed is the God and Father of our Lord Jesus Christ, who has blessed us with every spiritual blessing in the heavenly realms in Christ.

Truth Statement

I am blessed with every spiritual blessing in the heavenly places.

I want to start today's reading by repeating this promise: You *are* blessed with every spiritual blessing in the heavenly places. This is not a promise for the future, this is a promise for *now*. Please understand this promise is for us today, right at this very moment.

Like me, you are probably asking the question, "So what are the spiritual blessings?" For the last 20 days of this study, we will take a closer look at some of them together. And, we need to understand that we have access to these spiritual gifts. They are just that, a gift. And like any other gift, you need to take that gift from the giver and put it to use.

First off, Paul, the writer of Ephesians, is saying we should bless God because He has blessed us. This is true. We need to bless God with our words, our minds, our hearts, and our actions. He has *given* freely to us with the only requirement being that we be *in Christ*. If you have said "yes" to Jesus - confessed with your tongue that Jesus is Lord and believed in your heart that God raised Him from the dead - then you are *in Christ*.

As a born-again believer, you have been born into the Kingdom of vast riches, endless resources, and access to everything you will ever need to have an abundant life in Christ. As of this writing, Elon Musk is the wealthiest man in the world. Elon's wealth pales in comparison to God's riches and what you have access to. Because what God gives us is *priceless*.

In this context, Paul is essentially setting up the rest of his letter to the Ephesian church to outline and explain these very riches. From the knowledge *and* acceptance of these riches, we can live a life *fully alive in Christ!*

Much of the rest of this study deals with specific elements of these spiritual blessings, so do not stop now - read on!

When we understand these spiritual blessings and let them settle in our hearts and let the true desire of our lives - Godly, holy desires - flow out to others, we are fulfilling the Greatest Command. When we understand these spiritual blessings, we respond to God with adoration and praise for what He has done and what He has given us. We acknowledge Jesus as our King because of what He accomplished on the cross, how He conquered death through His resurrection, and the fact that He is seated at the Right Hand of the Father in Heaven. And we are seated in that place with Him. From this understanding and heart posture, we respond to God with love, adoration, praise, and worship. Then and only then, when we understand the spiritual blessings impact our identity, can we live our purpose in life - to love God and love others.

We must understand, however, that God does not necessarily promise material blessings. He promises spiritual blessings. But when we understand the spiritual blessings, many times the material blessings will follow. Why? Because we live a life void of fear, timidity, and doubt. This causes us to love others freely, and to go after life unashamed and full of grace (power), being driven by the love of Christ and our desire to be with Him forever. Once the fear is gone, and our hearts are healed, we are unstoppable.

Go today understanding that *every* spiritual blessing in Christ is yours for the taking! Jesus is giving them to you for free: Will you take them and steward over them well today and every day going forward? The choice is yours. Live free today knowing that you are in Christ and have been given *everything* you need to succeed in life!

Day 22

Ephesians 1:4

For he chose us in Christ before the foundation of the world that we may be holy and unblemished in his sight in love.

Truth Statement

I am chosen, holy, and blameless before God.

Today's verse is the root, the foundation, of our identity in Christ. It is a spiritual blessing, and it serves to be our foundation as we build our lives on the love of Christ. Why do we build our lives on the love of Christ? Ephesians 1:4 makes this clear - our response to God is love because He first loved us. He chose us. Stop and think about this for a moment. Not to dwell in the past, but all of us have messed up, walked away from God, or at least ignored Him. Yet He still chose us. He still loves us. He still pours out His love to us constantly. And He sees us, "in His sight," *in love.* This means that right now, because of His Son Jesus, God sees you. Whatever you are going through, whatever you are involved with, whatever you are ashamed of, He sees you. Even in your celebrations, when all is going well, in the middle of your success in life, He sees you.

And He loves you. He may not love your actions or thoughts or heart posture toward Him. But He still loves you anyway.

What does He say about you? "Son/daughter, I see you and I love you. Because of my love for you through which I gave up my one and only Son, Jesus, I see you as chosen, because you *are* chosen. I see you as holy because you *are* holy. I see you as blameless because you *are* blameless. I would not have seen you this way, except for the fact that my firstborn Son, Jesus, died for you. I gave Him up to death, so I could have *you.* I was the one that came up with the idea. Why would I allow such suffering and pain to happen to my Son? So that you would come back to me."

Today, turn back to God. Let's acknowledge God's love for us, the foundation of our identity, and live our lives like we believe it!

Repeat these words out loud today:

*I am chosen.*

*I am holy.*

*I am blameless.*

*In Christ.*

*Thank you, Jesus. Thank you, Daddy. I believe these truths about me, and today I will live my life differently, for you and your glory. Strengthen me today by reminding me of these truths all day, every day. Amen.*

Day 23

<u>Ephesians 1:7</u>

In him we have redemption through his blood, the forgiveness of our trespasses, according to the riches of his grace.

<u>Truth Statement</u>

I am forgiven by the grace of Christ.

You *have redemption.* You *are* forgiven. By grace. Do not speed read today. These words can go deep and pierce our hearts, if we allow this truth, these riches, to do so.

When Paul says, "In him," he is referring to Jesus. It is because of Jesus that any of this is possible. It is because of His love for you that He died for you on a cross, suffering an excruciating beating to the point of near-death, and then carrying His own cross upon which He was nailed and died. Temporarily. It is important to understand the promise of redemption and forgiveness in this context because there is a key word that we must first understand. That word is *grace.*

The riches that God pours out to us are based on grace. What is grace? Yes, it is unmerited favor for sure. But more importantly, grace is *power!* The word for grace in Greek is *"dunamis."* It is where we get the English word, dynamite. It is explosive power! It is a power that is so powerful, it raised Jesus from the dead. And this same power, this dunamis, is available to you.

If you have said "yes" to Jesus, you have dunamis in you already! You simply need to acknowledge it and allow it to be released through you, through the Holy Spirit in you.

Forgiveness is the next promise, the next element, in the riches of Christ. To be forgiven means that we have been released of the bondage or the price we should have to pay for our sins. Again, we are released, or free, because of Jesus and what He accomplished through His death, burial, and resurrection. But we must ask for forgiveness. What does this look like? It looks like this: Jesus, I know I have sinned. I admit it before you. Please forgive me.

At that moment, right when you sincerely confess your sins to Jesus, you are forgiven. Period. The Bible even says that Jesus keeps no record of the things we have done wrong and that our sins are as far as the east is from the west. This simply means that Jesus has completely, 100% decided to forget about the things you just asked forgiveness for. I write "decided" because forgiveness involves an intentional act for someone to take. And because Jesus chose you and loves you in a way that cannot be comprehended (Ephesians 3:19), your confession is accepted, Jesus has forgiven you, and Jesus has let go of the hurt you have caused Him, yourself, and possibly others.

Jesus has forgiven you. Now, will you live your life today like you are forgiven? This is *good news! This is freedom!* This is the *gospel*. Go and live your life today in the love and forgiveness of Jesus.

And when someone asks why you are so filled with joy today, be sure to tell them, "It is because of Jesus!"

Day 24

<u>Ephesians 1:11</u>

In him we have obtained an inheritance, having been predestined according to the purpose of him who works all things according to the counsel of his will…

<u>Truth Statement</u>

Because of Jesus, I am God's possession.

Today, we focus on more of the spiritual blessings that we have been given by God because of what His Son, Jesus, has done for us.

This verse begins with the words, "In him." Paul is referring to Jesus here. You are in Christ, and He is in you if you have said "yes" to Jesus. This is the starting point. Do not forget this truth about you! Your identity is in Christ and Christ alone!

Because of Jesus and the fact that He is in us and dwells in us through His Holy Spirit, God has claimed us as his possession. Because we are His possession, we are His inheritance, and we have access to His riches.

The way this sentence is structured in the Greek language, "we have obtained an inheritance," can also mean that "we are his inheritance."

Think about this for a moment. The Creator of the universe looks at you as His inheritance, His possession. He looks forward to the day where He will welcome you to heaven, the day when He will receive His full inheritance – you! That is incredible!

Have you ever received an inheritance? I have not, but I know people who have. While there typically is a loss associated with an inheritance, such as the passing of a loved one, when we die, God gets both us *and* His inheritance. Because of this, we are truly His possession, His *treasured* possession, a possession that He gave up his Son to receive.

The verse goes on to say, "…having been predestined." This sentence simply confirms the previous part of the same sentence. You were claimed, chosen by God, before you even knew it. When you said "yes" to Jesus, God knew you would. It is not a surprise to Him. He waited patiently for you. And now you are *His possession.*

Is there something that you possess that you would not give up, no matter what? Maybe it is a child, maybe it is a diamond ring, maybe it is your marriage or a friendship. The way you feel about that is the way God feels about you … times infinity! Remember, we cannot comprehend how much God loves us, but He does, more than we will *ever* know. Just believe it today. *You are loved by God!*

Day 25

<u>Ephesians 2:4-5</u>

But God, being rich in mercy, because of the great love with which he loved us, even when we were dead in our trespasses, made us alive together with Christ - by grace you have been saved!

<u>Truth Statement</u>

Because of God's mercy and love, I am saved and made alive with Christ.

Today we will continue to grow deeper in our understanding of the spiritual gifts that God lavishes upon us. God keeps giving and giving and giving and giving. He does not stop giving! He overwhelms me constantly with His love and mercy and spiritual gifts.

This passage starts with two important words, "But God..." There are those amazing words again. *But God. But God* was written by Paul because of what he wrote in the prior passages. It is kind of like the word, "therefore." If you see the word "therefore" you should ask what it is "there for." Paul is laying out his case for Christ by reminding us that we were living a life that was dead. Not physically dead, but spiritually dead. Paul says - and it is true of all of us - that we used to follow the ways of this world, the ways of Satan, our great enemy, giving in to any and all pleasures that came our way. Please understand that Paul is not saying we were knowingly doing this. Most of us just did not know. We were ignorant of the way we were living our lives. But that does not excuse us. We were still guilty of this fact.

But God ... because of His *great* love for us and because He is *rich* in mercy, *has made us alive together with Christ!*

So, what does this mean? Remember that it was God's idea to send His Son to this earth to suffer and endure all that He did. This God, our Father, gave up his Son *for you.* There was no other way to do it. He needed to come to earth, show and tell of the Kingdom, die, and be resurrected. That was God's plan, and it is perfect. It is because of this selfless act of love that you are saved. It is a done deal!

It may sound harsh to give up your only son. But let me ask you this - if you created all things, including all people, and you had to give up your firstborn son, knowing that He would be resurrected and return to you in heaven - for eternity - would you do it? What if you knew that by giving up your son you would have *many sons* with you, forever? What an incredibly unselfish act of love God has done for us.

And, not only are we saved, but we are *made alive with Christ.* This means literally "to reanimate conjointly with." Think about that for a moment. To reanimate something means that something has been restored to life and given fresh vigor. Conjointly means simply "to be joined together." So, another way to put this is that *we have been restored to life and given fresh vigor by being joined with Christ.*

Yes, we have truly been restored to life! We have been given fresh vigor! And this is because we have Christ in us, the Holy Spirit, and we are literally joined together with Him. We are one with Him. There is no way to separate that love of Jesus in us (Romans 8:38-39).

Today, rejoice! Because of God's love and mercy for you, you are saved and made alive in Christ!

Day 26

Colossians 3:1

Therefore, if you have been raised with Christ, keep seeking the things above, where Christ is, seated at the right hand of God.

Truth Statement

Because I am raised up with Christ, I have been given His authority.

As we approach the end of this 40-day study of our new identity in Christ, my prayer for you is that you are starting to live your life more confidently *in and through Jesus!* We do not live our lives in our own strength and ability but in the strength and ability of Jesus, who is in us and who pours out of us toward others.

Today, we stay on the topic of authority. Knowing *who* we are in Christ, and *where* we are in Christ, is key to understanding our *authority* in Christ.

Paul starts this passage by saying, "if you have been raised with Christ." He is differentiating those who believe this and those who do not. If you have said "yes" to Jesus, you have died to this world, and you have been resurrected in the spiritual realm and are seated with Jesus at the Right Hand of God. Again, we are not Jesus, and we are not God, but we have been invited to sit *with Jesus* in this place of authority.

Because we are raised with Christ, Paul says, "keep seeking the things above, where Christ is." Let's break this down today, so we can fully understand what Paul is saying and go deeper into our identity and authority in Christ.

"Keep seeking" means "to seek after something in order to find it, by thinking and praying." It also is translated as "to *crave* something and to *demand* something from someone."

"Things above" simply means the things of God. And for us in this context, it strongly urges us to keep seeking after our identity in Christ, who we are, and who God says we are. We must *keep seeking after this to the point of craving it and demanding that we understand it!*

What Paul has written, and what I am emphasizing, is that we are to *never, ever give up!* Jesus did not die for us to quit. Ever. We are not quitters, we

58

are fighters! Keep seeking after the truths of Jesus so that you find them. Think about them. Pray about them. And crave - no, *demand* - that you find them. This *demanding* is a type of self-talk you need to perform over yourself every day of your life. When you feel like giving up, when your mind starts to wander, demand your mind to get back on track.

I once heard a pastor say, "You'll never overcome thoughts with thoughts." This is true. You cannot think your way into battling against thoughts. You must *speak out the battle, the spiritual gifts, the truths of Jesus, your identity over yourself. Every day!*

So today, let's put this into practice. When thoughts come into your mind that you no longer want to entertain, say out loud, *"In the name of Jesus, I take this thought captive and send it back to the abyss where it belongs! Instead, I think about my authority, Jesus, that place where I am now sitting, at the Right Hand of God, and where I am also seated with You, Jesus. I have the same authority that you have. And because of this, I take authority over all thoughts that are not from you, in Jesus' name! Amen!"*

As you grow in the understanding of your true identity, this prayer will become second nature to you. But never forget the power of your spoken words. When doubt, fear, warfare, regrets, or anxiety comes your way, take authority over it and declare it gone and abolished forever, in Jesus' name!

Day 27

<u>Ephesians 2:6</u>

And he raised us up with him and seated us with him in the heavenly places in Christ Jesus.

<u>Truth Statement</u>

I am seated in the heavenly places with Christ.

Hang on and hold on tight. Today's message about identity is going to absolutely blow your mind - again! It is from this particular spiritual gift of God that we find our *authority*.

Right now, at this very moment, and in every moment of the rest of your life, you *are seated in the heavenly places with Jesus*. It is true. You are. Right now. So, what does this mean?

If you remember from Day 25, we were once dead in our transgressions. Go back and review that if necessary. But this means that we were spiritually dead and not filled with the Holy Spirit, and we were walking in the ways of the world, not the ways of Jesus.

Then, we were saved! Woohoo! We have received the gifts of mercy and grace, and the gift of salvation. Then, we were filled with the Holy Spirit. This caused us to be one with Jesus Himself. Because we are one with Jesus, we are in the same place where He is, right now, and He is in the place where we are, right now. This is a unique, powerful spiritual gift unlike any other.

Let's break this down a bit more. Jesus, via the Holy Spirit, is in us. We are one with Jesus. Yes, He is with us, but that also means, logically, that we are with Him. You cannot be seated next to someone without that person being seated next to you. That is impossible. Because of this, we are seated with Jesus, where He is.

So, where is He? He is in heaven, seated right next to and at the Right Hand of God. He is seated in the place of authority, ruling and reigning over everything as the King of kings and the Lord of lords. And there you are, right next to Jesus. Also ruling and reigning. Now, we are not the King, but we are kings. We are not Lord, but we are lords.

I do not have time to explain this in detail, but heaven is not a place we go and suddenly sprout wings and play harps all day long, floating around in the clouds. No. The Bible says heaven will be here on earth, and we will rule and reign over it. Now, God's Kingdom has come, *and* it has yet to come. Again, I cannot go into detail, but it is true. You have the Holy Spirit, Jesus, in you. Therefore, you have the Kingdom of God in you. The Kingdom of God is *now*. And Jesus has asked us to rule and reign as kings (this is true for women, too). Today. On this earth. At this moment. With the authority that has been given to us by Jesus, because we have been raised with Him.

Remember this is a spiritual gift, one that you must grasp and take hold of. There are a lot of Christians that do not know this truth and live their lives not utilizing the full authority and power they have been given. Do not make that mistake.

One more thing. Because we are seated next to Jesus spiritually, we can see things from a spiritual perspective. This means that we can and should see situations and people from Jesus' perspective. If we are seated with Him, we can see what He sees. When I pray, I envision what it might look like where Jesus is seated. Then, as I approach this throne, I take my seat next to Jesus. From there I can see myself and my situation from Jesus' perspective. This has been a game-changer for me. I encourage you to do the same every time you pray.

Today, start living with the authority of Jesus that is rightfully yours (because you have been raised and are seated with Christ) to help fulfill your purpose in life today - to love God and to love others well.

Day 28

<u>Ephesians 2:10</u>

For we are his workmanship, created in Christ Jesus for good works, which God prepared beforehand, that we should walk in them.

<u>Truth Statement</u>

I am God's workmanship created to produce good works.

The spiritual gifts keep coming and coming! Yahweh is such a giving, kind, and loving God! Today focuses on the "how" and the "why" of our identity. If you recall, the book I wrote titled, *Identity-Driven Purpose,* is all about how we see ourselves and how we live our lives with greater purpose. Today's verse gives us the fuel to do this well.

This verse starts with the words "For we are his workmanship." This simply means that we were made by Him. Have you ever made something with your own hands? Perhaps you are a carpenter or builder. Or maybe you like to make crafts with your children. Or maybe gardening is your hobby. Whatever it is, we have all created something with our own hands. Does it not feel good when we finish building it? This is how God feels about you. In Genesis 1:31, God looked at all He had made, including man, and said it was "very good." God says you are *very good,* and He is pleased with what He made. He made you. Stop for a moment and thank Him for creating you. Why? Read on.

We were created "in Christ Jesus." This means that Jesus was there. Jesus has been with His Father since the beginning of everything. He was there when you were created. He oversaw and participated in your creation. The only time in history when Jesus was not with His Father was when Jesus came to earth as a baby and lived apart from God for 33 years. However, Jesus said He did not do anything He did not see His Father doing, so Jesus was still intimately connected to His Father even though Jesus was apart from Him.

Further, the text reads "created...for good works." You were created to do great things, to do good in all you do, whatever you do. In fact, Paul takes this further in Colossians 3:23, where he writes that whatever you do, do it well as if you are doing it for God.

Whatever you do. I think this has dual meanings. There is your day job, whatever you do for a living. Then there are the good works of loving others. Love God, love others. God created us to do this, and He has given us everything we need to succeed at both, our "paying" job and our "loving" job.

God made us unique in His image for a specific thing - to honor Him in all we do, all day, every day. He knows the situations you face, and He knows your challenges. But He has given you everything you need to accomplish everything He has for you. *He has prepared you for the things He has prepared for you to do.*

Today, go and do what you do, do it well, and do it all for God. There is nothing you will face today that you are not prepared for. Trust in the Holy Spirit to lead you through everything, including your purpose in life - loving God and loving others well.

Day 29

Ephesians 2:13

But now in Christ Jesus you who once were far off have been brought near by the blood of Christ.

Truth Statement

I am brought near to God by the blood of Christ.

Today we are going to go over what it means to have been rescued, and to receive the intimacy and *access* that follows. Colossians 1:13 says that God rescued us from the kingdom of darkness and transferred us into the Kingdom of His Son Jesus. Because God loves us so much, He rescued us. Some of you may be thinking that you did not need to be rescued. I would say that you did. We all did. There was our life before Jesus and our life now with Jesus. They should be two different lives - one that was dead spiritually, living in darkness, and one that is now alive and living in the light.

We have been rescued. Like a life raft thrown to a person who is drowning, God came to our rescue and saved us from death - both spiritual and literal. We have talked about spiritual death already. But literal death has also been overcome. Yes, we will die in these mortal bodies that God created for us. But once we die our physical death, we spend eternity with God in heaven.

Because we have been rescued by God, we have been brought near to Him through the blood of Christ. Like we covered in earlier days of this study, the death, burial, and resurrection of Jesus - His "blood" - completely paid the price for the penalty we should have paid for our sins, the ways we have missed the mark. Just a few days ago, on Day 27, we talked about being raised with Christ and the fact that we are seated with Him in the heavenly places.

Today's spiritual blessing is intimacy with Christ, access to, and closeness with our Daddy in heaven, all because He came to our rescue and transferred us into His Kingdom, His reality. This is a beautiful picture that displays God's love for us. It is a wonderful image of the great lengths, and for many of us, the incredible patience, that God went to find us, wake us up, and carry us into His Kingdom.

We are near to God because first, He is in us. We have His Holy Spirit in us who searches the depths of our Father's heart. Second, we are near to God because we are seated next to Him, in the heavenly places. If needed, go back and read Day 27's passage again.

Today, spend some time thanking and worshiping God for the tremendous power and love He has shown us by coming after us, time after time, and rescuing us from ourselves and from the enemy, and bringing us close, *so close* to Him that we are literally filled with His Spirit and seated right next to him. Always and forever.

Day 30

Ephesians 3:6

The Gentiles are fellow heirs, members of the same body, and partakers of the promise in Christ Jesus.

Truth Statement

I am a member of Christ's body and a partaker of His promise.

Unless you are Jewish, you are a Gentile. This is not a bad thing; in fact, it is a blessing. Why? Because for those of us who have said "yes" to Jesus, we have the same inheritance, and the same fellowship, and the same promises that were given to the Jews, starting with Abraham way back in the Old Testament times. You see, God made the original covenant with Abraham, a promise that nations and kings would descend from him. It is an amazing story, one that needs to be read if you have not already done so. The story is found in the book of Genesis.

Because the promise was originally given to God's people, the Israelites, the Jews, for thousands of years it was a covenant with them only. But God sent His Son Jesus to reconcile *all people* to Himself. This is great news! This is the gospel! Because of what Jesus accomplished through His death, burial, and resurrection, we are also heirs to God's riches, we are members of His family, the Church, and we are partakers of His promise - eternity with Him.

This spiritual blessing, being an heir, a fellow member of the Church, and partakers in God's promise, is beyond measure. And for this, we should respond with love, adoration, and worship of God, every day.

Whether or not you currently attend a church, if you have said "yes" to Jesus, you are a member of His body. And like we discussed two days ago, God has given you specific skills and abilities to enable you to participate in His good purposes for His glory. Some of these skills should be used with others, as a group. God does not intend for us to be alone. He created us for relationship. Because of this, we should be in a loving, healthy, dynamic relationship with God and with others. If we are not, how can we fulfill our purpose in life, loving others?

Today, reflect on your relationships and whether or not you are part of a

66

loving and accepting community with other believers in Jesus Christ. If you are, how can you love them (and everyone you encounter today) well? If you are not, prayerfully consider taking a step toward being part of a church that teaches the truth of Jesus from the Bible.

Make an effort to go deeper in this journey with fellow believers today.

Day 31

Ephesians 3:12

…in whom we have boldness and confident access to God because of Christ's faithfulness.

Truth Statement

I have boldness and confident access to God through faith in Christ.

Two days ago, we briefly discussed the concept of having bold access to God. Today's spiritual blessing amplifies and solidifies our identity and purpose in one single verse! Let me explain.

Through Jesus, we have "boldness and confident access" to God. We cannot bypass the fact that all of these spiritual blessings are *because* of Jesus, are accessed *through* Jesus, and are to be used *for* Jesus and His glory. Thank You, Jesus!

Boldness. This word can take on a lot of meanings, but it is typified through people's actions. We say things like, "Wow, that was bold!" or "Man, you took a bold step today." While these may be true, this is not exactly what the word in this context means. The Greek word for boldness is *"parresia,"* which means, "freedom in speaking, unreservedness in speech; speaking openly and frankly, without concealment; speaking without ambiguity; having free and fearless confidence, cheerful courage, and assurance."

Confidence. Similar to boldness, we often look at people and comment on their confidence in life, perhaps the way they go after life without fear. This is an accurate description of the word in this context. The Greek word for confident is *"pepoithesis,"* which means simply "trust, confidence, reliance."

The word *access* in this passage means "moving to or approaching." Let's take a look at this phrase with these new definitions:

*I have the freedom to speak, and I am invited to speak openly and frankly to God, without concealing anything. I do not need to fear coming to God and saying what I want or need to say. I can move toward God and approach Him not only without fear, but confidently trusting that He sees me and hears me.*

The Book of Psalms reveals that King David understood this. The Psalms mirror this definition well. David often poured his heart out toward God. You see it throughout the Psalms that he wrote.

Did the expansion of the meaning of this spiritual blessing make it more meaningful for you? I hope so. Because this spiritual blessing truly is the basis of our identity and our purpose in life. Think about it. We can approach God, the Creator of the universe, at any time, in any place, with utmost confidence and assurance that we can talk to Him about *anything.* Anything! It is an invitation that is unlike any other!

There is one more important aspect to this verse that I must mention. While we do have bold, confident access to God, this does not mean that we should do all the talking. Since we can approach God, we should listen to what He wants to say to us. Sometimes, the best prayer we can pray is the prayer of silence before Him. It is in these quiet times when the still, small voice of God speaks to us.

Today, do not move on from here without approaching God confidently and boldly. Speak to Him about anything and everything that is on your mind, anything and everything that you want Him to hear. Then listen. And here is the blessing in all of this … this is not for Him. It is for *you!* God knows you want to approach Him, but as we discussed on an earlier day, as we draw near to Him, He draws near to us, and He hears us. He loves us despite our failures and faults. So, approach Him today confidently and boldly and watch how your love for God and love for others begins to be magnified.

Day 32

Ephesians 4:24

Put on the new man who has been created in God's image - in righteousness and holiness that comes from truth.

Truth Statement

I am a new man (woman) who is righteous and holy.

In the Bible, many times when you see statements like "you are a son" it is referring to both men and women, so if you are a woman, do not feel left out. These truths are just as much for you as they are for men.

Put on the new man. What?! What on earth is Paul talking about here? Putting on a new man sounds very strange. Consider it this way. Think about a homeless man that you have seen in your city. He typically has some ragged clothes and is not necessarily showered and shaved and ready to enter into society. Then imagine this. Someone comes along, offers him the promise of a new life if he would just put on some new clothes. He is given a nice Armani suit and directions on how to get to his interview for a job that will more than pave his way toward a new life. So, he strips down, puts on the new clothes, and then puts on the old, tattered clothes right on top of the Armani suit.

Ridiculous, right? Nobody would do that! Yet, it is what many of us do every day. God has given us a new heart (Ezekiel 36:26) when we said "yes" to Jesus. This means that we are a new creation in Christ. We are a new man, a new woman, with a new purpose, a new outlook, and a new focus in life: loving God and loving others.

But many of us either forget or purposefully neglect the gift of our new heart, our new man, and we go on living the same way we did before we said "yes" to Jesus. This is a travesty because we all have the path to life - putting on the new man. So, what does this mean?

It is really simple. What you are doing here, by going through *A 40-Day Journey to Your New Identity in Christ* is putting on the new man. What "putting on the new man" entails is simply reminding yourself of who you are in Christ and living that out every day. Unfortunately, with everything that inundates us daily, we tend to go back to our old ways, our learned habits, the "easy" way of life, and forget who we are and the authority we have in Christ.

Putting on the new man is a powerful, spiritual truth that is often neglected. I believe it is neglected because of the second part of this passage, the part about "holiness." We see the word *holiness,* and we say to ourselves that living a holy life is not possible. I would agree - apart from Christ. However, the Bible says:

- I can do all things through Christ who strengthens me (Philippians 4:13).
- Be holy, for I am holy (1 Peter 1:16).
- Even the least among you can do all that I have done, and greater things (John 14:12).

God is calling us to a higher standard, not one of perfection, but one of holiness. This means we are to be blameless before God. And you know what? Apart from Christ, that is impossible. However, with Christ, with the new man put on, it is possible. How? Through Christ's sacrifice and forgiveness. Period. We are seen as holy in the eyes of God because of what Jesus did.

Today, put on the new man and do not cover him up! Remember who you are, whose you are, where you are (seated next to Jesus), and live your life in the power of Christ!

Day 33

Philippians 3:20

But our citizenship is in heaven - and we also await a savior from there, the Lord Jesus Christ.

Truth Statement

I am a citizen of heaven.

Yesterday, we were reminded to put on the new man. Today, we take that concept a step further to remind ourselves about our *position* in Christ, our *citizenship* in Christ.

You may be a citizen of the United States, Canada, Italy, or another country. But you are a citizen of heaven first. In order to understand this, we need to understand a concept that is not talked about very much today - the concept of "kingdom."

A kingdom is simply a geographic area that is ruled and reigned by a king. There are many kingdoms around today, Bahrain, Cambodia, Jordan, and Morocco, just to name several. These kingdoms are ruled and reigned by an individual, otherwise known as a monarchy, where one individual holds the most power.

There is also the Kingdom of Heaven. This Kingdom encompasses all of the earth and the universe. It is ruled and reigned by Jesus (Matthew 28:18). This is good news, because this same all-powerful, all-knowing, Supreme Being is the same Person that died on a cross - for you. When you said "yes" to Jesus, you were immediately adopted into this family, and you became a citizen of this Kingdom, where Jesus is the King of kings and Lord of lords.

Another important concept to understand is the idea of ambassadorship. Every country in the world has ambassadors from their country that live and serve in other countries. Their goal is to represent their home country *as if they were the president or leader.* They are not the president or leader, but they have been sent by their president or leader to represent them in the affairs of their country or kingdom.

This is *exactly* what God has done for us. He has appointed us to be ambassadors to our kingdoms, our areas of influence, as if we are Him. Remember, we will never be God, but with the Holy Spirit in us, we can - and should - represent Him well as a citizen of heaven. This means everywhere we go, everyone we talk to, as we go about our days, we are to represent God and the Kingdom of God. Since we carry that citizenship, that Kingdom with us everywhere we go, we should represent Him well.

Ambassadorship also comes with authority from the leader or president. Jesus has given *you* authority to represent, to speak on His behalf, to forgive, to heal, to pray, to do everything Jesus does - and more!

Finally, ambassadorship comes with special protections, immunities, and rights. In most countries, as an ambassador from another country, you are immune from certain laws, protected against violence and harm, and given rights that citizens of that country do not have. It is the same as an ambassador for Christ - and more! You have access to the Armor of God for protection (Ephesians 6). You are immune to the influence and stain of this world. You are sacred and inviolable as a son or daughter of the King! And just as ambassadors have the right to herald opinions of their nation, you have the right to share the Good News of Jesus everywhere you go!

The citizenship of heaven trumps all other citizenship. You are a citizen of heaven first, and a citizen of your earthly nation second. This may be why you sometimes feel like a "fish out of water" in your life. You may feel alone at times. Just know, back home, there is a great cloud of witnesses cheering you on at every moment of every day (Hebrews 12:1)!

So today, go out knowing that you are a citizen of heaven with all authority to make disciples of all nations: Be bold and be strong and be courageous today. Your citizenship in heaven is solidified, certified, and fortified in Christ Jesus!

Day 34

Philippians 4:7

And the peace of God that surpasses all understanding will guard your hearts and minds in Christ Jesus.

Truth Statement

The peace of God guards my heart and mind.

Today brings forth a spiritual blessing so instrumental in our lives that this single passage alone has the power to change the way you live forever!

Yesterday we discussed being ambassadors for Christ. Being an ambassador in a foreign land comes with uncertainties and fears. You may speak a language that is foreign to everyone around you. You may look different, too. Yet you have been sent by your person of authority to represent, protect, and even influence policy for your homeland.

The same is true as an ambassador for Christ. Being an ambassador for Christ will come with its own set of challenges, communication difficulties, and assignments. But here is the difference. As an ambassador of a country from this world, you do not have your leader with you. As an ambassador for Christ, you have the King with you - always! And this fact alone should bring about a peace that allows you to flourish in life.

What is the peace that Paul is talking about in this passage? The meaning of "peace" is this:

- A state of national tranquility - exemption from the rage and havoc of war
- Peace between individuals
- Security, safety, prosperity
- A tranquil state of a soul assured of its salvation in Christ

I do not know about you, but I want all of those! Interestingly, this peace, while it is available to us, it is something we *must embrace and take hold of.* Jesus says in John 14:27, "My peace I leave with you; my peace I give to you." This peace is real; it actually exists because Jesus had it, and He has left it for us as a gift. He has given *His peace* to us. But just as you receive a gift from a friend for your birthday, you must take it, open it, and not only acknowledge it, but put it to use. You must believe that you have this peace, you must say that you have this peace, and you must remember that you have this peace. You must renew your mind with this peace.

Notice the first definition of peace above. It says "exemption from" not "taken away from." This means that you are exempt, through the peace of Jesus, from the damage, rage, and the havoc of war. It will not come to you and your house - if you remain in the peace of Jesus - in Jesus' name!

I urge you to go right now and read Psalm 91. This particular psalm talks about how to embrace God's peace and receive its benefits.

This "exemption" from the damages of war is exactly what this passage is referring to when it says that this peace will "guard your hearts and minds in Christ Jesus." The word *guard* is a military term. Paul is saying we are in a war! But God's peace guards us against the damages of war. This word *guard* means to, "protect by a military guard, to prevent hostile invasion." WOW! As we abide in Christ, we remain close to Him. Remember, if we draw near to Him, He will draw near to us, *and we will have this peace that guards our hearts and minds!*

So right now, stop. Take a deep breath. Say to yourself, out loud, *"I have the peace of God that guards my heart and my mind in you, Jesus. Thank you, Jesus. In the midst of all that I struggle with in life, you have a guard around my heart and my mind. There will not be a hostile invasion of my heart and mind, in the name of Jesus! The damages of the war that I am currently fighting will not come near me. I am exempt from all the damages that this world and the enemy want to inflict on me. In Jesus' name. Amen."*

Today, step out in boldness and with courage knowing that your heart and mind are guarded through the peace of Jesus. Embrace the peace of God today!

Day 35

<u>Philippians 4:19</u>

God will supply your every need according to his glorious riches in Christ Jesus.

<u>Truth Statement</u>

God supplies all my needs.

Today's focus is about trust. This spiritual blessing, the fact that God supplies *all* of our needs, is profound. The needs we all have as followers of Christ are met through the *riches* of Christ. We covered the topic of His riches earlier in this study on Days 21 and 23.

As we have been diving deeper into our identity and the importance of hanging onto and believing with everything that is in us about God's promises for us, it is important to understand that today's verse is no different. At the end of the day, it all comes down to faith and trust. Do you believe the promises of God, and are you going to grasp them as if they are your own? Because they are yours. You just have to believe and take hold of them.

Let's break down this verse, so we can fully understand what Paul has written. It is important to take a close look at every word, including words like "will supply." In English, these are two separate words. In the Greek language, the language in which this letter was originally written, it is one word *"pleroo."* It is a verb, an action word, which means "to make full, to fill up, to fill to the full, to cause to abound, and to furnish and supply liberally." It also means "I abound, and I am filled up" and "to complete."

This passage has a dual meaning: Paul is saying that not only has God supplied all of *his* needs, He will *also supply all of your needs!* Paul has experienced it, so he knows it is true, and he is passing along his experience and the promise of God to us.

Let's look at the next set of words. "Every need" is also translated as "all your needs." This is important to understand as well.

"All" means "individually, each, every, any, all, everyone." This verse applies to everyone *who is in Christ Jesus.* For those who have not said "yes" to Jesus, this may not apply. However, for those of us who have said "yes" to Jesus, this is a *promise!*

"Need" means "necessity, duty, or business." Now let's take a look at exactly what this promise is for us.

God promises to *fill you up with everything you need, even to overflowing, with all that is necessary for you to succeed at your work, at whatever you do in life.* We must understand these verses in their context. Paul is talking about his work, his ministry, and how he has been supplied with everything he has needed, in good times and in bad. Philippians 4:13 is also where we find the promise, "I can do all things through Him who strengthens me."

Read carefully. Paul is not saying God is going to give you everything you *want* in life. He is saying from experience that God will supply you with everything you need to perform the duties that God has assigned to you *well, and with excellence.* This ties directly into Colossians 3:17, where Paul writes, "And whatever you do, in word or deed, do it all in the name of the Lord Jesus, giving thanks to God the Father through Him." We all have things that we do in life. Whatever it is that you do, do it as unto the Lord and glorify Him with it. When we live our lives for the glory of God, He will fully supply and equip our every need.

Here is my question to you: What do you do? Do you go to work every day somewhere? Are you a stay-at-home mom or dad? Are you unemployed? *Whatever you do*, God will supply everything you need to succeed at what you do. This is a promise.

Go today with a full understanding that God will fill you to overflowing in your life so that you can be successful and give Him the glory for it all!

Day 36

Colossians 2:10

You have been filled in him, who is the head over every ruler and authority.

Truth Statement

I am made complete in Christ.

The spiritual gifts just keep pouring in! I hope that you are getting a clearer picture that when we find our identity in Jesus Christ, our drive in life, what we do, and the way we love others fulfills our purpose in life. And God supplies everything we need to live a life full of loving God and loving others. This is your *Identity-Driven Purpose* in life!

Today's focus is about authority. If you recall, back on Day 27, we talked about our *position* in Christ, the fact that we are seated with Him in the heavenly places. Today's verse starts with the words, "you have been filled in him." Remember, if you have said "yes" to Jesus, you *are filled with Him!* In the King James version of the Bible, this verse reads, "and in Him you have been made complete." By now you should have this truth fully sealed in your mind and heart. You have the Holy Spirit in you, which means you are filled with Jesus, and you *are complete!* You lack nothing, your life matters, and you have an identity and a purpose in life that transcends every obstacle and stumbling block this world tries to throw at you. You are *filled,* and you are *complete!*

The second part of the verse reads, "who is head over every ruler and authority." This is really important to understand. Please read carefully and take your time today to fully understand what was written about you here.

The phrase "head over" in English is two words. Again, in Greek, it is a single word *"kephale."* This word derives itself from the root word *"kapto,"* which means something has been seized. The word *"kephale"* goes on to mean a literal head of something, like the head on your shoulders. Further, it is also defined as the one who is supreme, chief, or one who is prominent. Finally, it also is interpreted as "cornerstone."

Many of you have probably sung the song "Cornerstone" by Hillsong. This is the truth of Jesus you are singing about. He is the Head, the Cornerstone, the Supreme or Prominent One. The point is this: Jesus is supreme. Over what? I'm glad you asked.

"Every ruler and authority." This is where it gets really good! "Ruler" in Greek means, "beginning, the first person in a series, a leader, that by which anything begins, and angels and demons." So, let's set things straight. Jesus is the head, the supreme, the #1 ruler over all people, time, leaders, the beginning of all things, *and angels and demons.* He has authority over all demons. Period. They all must bow at His command. Let's move on.

"Authority" means, from the Greek, "physical and mental power, the power of authority (influence) and of right (privilege), government, any crown or sign that is used as authority." Paul is saying that there is no person or authority figure or government that is above Jesus. Jesus is Head over it all.

So, let's take a look at how we could say this sentence now that we know what is being written here: *You are filled and complete in Jesus who is the head, the supreme leader of everything, every person, every government, everything. There is nothing that Jesus is not head over.*

Now, let's take one step further. Because we are seated with Jesus in the heavenly places, we too have access to this same authority. Let me be very clear about something here: We are not Jesus. We are not God. We cannot and will not attain that status. Ever. However, we can tap into that power and utilize that authority to glorify God in all we do, all day and every day. Paul is saying, "You can do it!"

As Paul writes in Colossians 2:8, nothing can take us captive by philosophy and empty deceit, according to human tradition. Nothing and no one.

Today, see to it that you stay rooted and grounded in Jesus Christ. Be filled and complete, and love God and love others with all authority and all power, in Christ Jesus!

Day 37

<u>Colossians 3:3</u>

For you have died and your life is hidden with Christ in God.

<u>Truth Statement</u>

My life is hidden with Christ in God.


Today, we are going to plunge deep into the depths of Christ's love for us. We have been journeying through our identity in Christ and our purpose in life, and today we go to a place of solitude and rest. Much of our identity and purpose in life will face a constant battle. There is a battle in our minds, there is a battle in our relationships. Everywhere we look and everywhere we turn, life can be a struggle.

And there are times when we just need to stop and rest in the arms of God. This is where we are going today. Take a deep breath and let it all out. God is with you right now.

We need to start where Paul began in this sentence: We have died. This is not physical death. Paul is saying that we have died to the influences of this world, and there is nothing this world can do to us. Nothing. We have the Holy Spirit in us, and as Paul says in Hebrews 13:6, "What can man do to me?" We have nothing and no one to fear. This should comfort us and allow us to live in the authority with which Christ has filled us.

As I mentioned above, because we are constantly battling against ourselves and the things of this world, and the things in the spiritual world, we need rest every now and then. Paul knew this, which is why he wrote the words "your life is hidden with Christ in God."

Reminder: Jesus is the head authority person over *everything and everyone.* And Jesus is seated right next to the Creator of the universe, God. And we have been raised with Christ. Therefore, we are safe in His presence, so safe that Paul says we are "hidden." What does this mean?

The Greek word for "hidden" is *"krypto,"* and this is where we get the word *cryptography.* In the computer world, as many of you know, there are constant attacks against corporations and computers globally, almost continually. Companies have been formed to supply users and organizations with ways to protect their data. This is usually referred to as "encrypting your data." When your data is encrypted, thieves try to access and steal your data, but they cannot because your data is hidden or put into a language that they cannot understand. That is exactly the idea here.

Because we are hidden in Christ, we are hidden *in God*. King David puts it this way in Psalm 91:1, "Whoever dwells in the shelter of the Most High will rest in the shadow of the Almighty." Because we dwell with Jesus, we live in the shelter of God, in His shadow, the shadow of the Almighty!

And it is in this place, in the shadow of God, in His shelter, we rest.

Today, take a deep breath and rest. Before you head out for your day, or to your next meeting, or to pick up your kids from school, or to that job interview, rest. You are hidden with Christ in God. There is *nothing this world can do to harm you.*

Rest today in the shadow of Almighty God.

Day 38

Colossians 3:4

When Christ (who is your life) appears, then you too will be revealed in glory with him.

Truth Statement

Christ is my life, and I will be revealed with Him in glory.

Today, we focus on the second coming of Christ. Jesus will return someday. This is a promise. However, this is not a concept that is easily understood. But here are some scriptures that confirm Jesus' return.

John 14:1-3 says, "Let not your heart be troubled. In My Father's house are many mansions; if it were not so, I would have told you. I go to prepare a place for you. And if I go and prepare a place for you, I will come again and receive you to Myself; that where I am, there you may be also."

Matthew 24:27 says, "For as the lightning comes from the east and shines as far as the west, so will be the coming of the Son of Man."

The fact of the matter, as we get closer to the end of our 40-day journey together, is that Jesus is going to return. We do not know when, but He will. And when He does, you will be revealed in glory with Him.

What does this mean? It is the promise of eternity with Jesus, with our restored bodies, ruling and reigning with Him forever because of what Jesus did for you. He died for you so that not only can you live in fullness in this life on this earth at this moment, but that you will be revealed with Him in heaven before the Father, spotless and blameless on that great and marvelous day!

So how does this apply to us today? Eternity with Jesus relates to what we studied yesterday, that we are hidden with Christ in God. Protected by Him, we shake off all fear and timidity, and we live our lives *on purpose* and *with purpose* because *we know who we are in Christ*. In many ways, eternity culminates in everything we've traveled through together these past 38 days. We live this life in the fullness of our identity and purpose, utilizing all the spiritual gifts that have been given to us, to battle and fight for the Kingdom every day. And on that day, we will be revealed with Christ in heaven, and these words will be spoken over us, "Well done, my good and faithful servant!"

Today, know that eternity awaits. And may that drive your life of *Identity-Driven Purpose* today and every day!

Day 39

Colossians 3:12

Therefore, as the elect of God, holy and dearly loved, clothe yourselves with a heart of mercy, kindness, humility, gentleness, and patience.

Truth Statement

I am filled with mercy, kindness, humility, gentleness, and patience.

My prayer for you today is that your life is truly different, that the fullness of your identity, your drivenness, and your purpose is coming alive within you!

I do not need to tell you that you are loved by God. By now that love should be anchored deeply within your heart! So now let's talk about clothing ourselves with a heart of mercy, kindness, humility, gentleness, and patience. This is the part of our identity that we live out every day - loving others. Remember the Greatest Command? Love God and love others.

However, Paul takes it to a place deep, deep within us. Our bowels. What?! Yes, our bowels. Now, for us in this day, we may not fully understand how things were written 2,000 years ago, yet it applies just as much to us today as it did to people back then.

Paul is saying to clothe ourselves with "a heart of" mercy. The Greek word for heart here is "*splagchnon.*" It is a pretty crazy word! The root of the word "heart" is where we get our word "spleen." It also means "bowels, intestines, heart, lungs, and liver."

Paul is describing the deepest, most inward parts of our being. These deep, inner parts of our soul are what the Bible also describes as the "seat of our passions," love, and anger. Paul is saying that in this place we need to clothe ourselves with mercy.

Paul is exhorting us to fill ourselves with these attributes, to the point where everything inside of us, in every element of our bodies, our very makeup, every essence of who we are, should pour out mercy, kindness, humility, gentleness, and patience.

The word "mercy" here is also the word for *compassion*. Jesus poured out compassion upon everyone He met. For example, Matthew 9:36 says, "When he saw the crowds, he had compassion for them, because they were harassed and helpless, like sheep without a shepherd." It is this compassion of Jesus that took Him to the cross to die for them, and for you and me. Compassion should derive itself from deep within us as we live our lives purposefully loving others well.

The meaning of the word "kindness" means integrity. Be integrous in all you do and clothe yourself with integrity.

"Humility" means to have a humble opinion of one's self. In other words, get rid of pride! The Bible says that God opposes the proud (Proverbs 3:34 and James 4:6). I do not have the space to go into the depths of pride, but please know that God resists those who are proud.

"Gentleness" can also be described as meek. Not weak, but meek. Jesus said He was meek in that He needed His Father in heaven. Jesus said that He did not do anything that He did not see or hear the Father doing or saying. To be meek means to be totally dependent on God and God alone.

And finally, "patience." This word means to have endurance, to be consistent, to persevere, and to be slow in avenging wrongs.

Another way to write this verse would be as follows: *Loved children of God, today and every day, clothe yourself with compassion and integrity, exuding humbleness while you lean completely on Jesus for all your needs, patiently persevering in all things, being slow to pay someone back for hurting you.*

Today, as you go about your day, listen to the inner depths of yourself. As you sense compassion, mercy, kindness, humility, gentleness, and patience wanting to pour out toward others, let it. No fear, no timidity. Allow love for others to drive your purpose today!

Day 40

<u>1 Thessalonians 1:4</u>

We know, brothers and sisters loved by God, that he has chosen you.

<u>Truth Statement</u>

God loves me.


Wow! What a journey this has been! My prayer for you is this: that you now see God, yourself, and others differently, and that your life is fully alive knowing your identity is in Christ, your drivenness is based on compassion, and that your purpose in life is to love God and love others well.

So today we end where we started - in God's love. 1 Thessalonians 1:4 is a simple passage that needs no explanation at this point in our journey. We end on the most important aspect of your life: God loves you.

When things do not go your way, when life throws you a curveball, when relationships do not work out, and when you are feeling anxious and alone, know that God loves you, and He is with you. Always.

Go today in God's love. You know how to do this now. You are a new creation in Christ. You now understand your new identity. You are loved. Go out into the world, loving God and others well!

## Conclusion

My prayer for you is that this study truly has changed your life. May you see yourself and others the way God sees you and others, as loved children of God.

I mentioned briefly in a few of the studies about warfare. Trust me - we are in a battle that is more dangerous than we may realize. If we could pull back the curtain of heaven and see the constant war that is raging for us and this world, we would be terrified. But God has given us not a spirit of fear but a Spirit of power, love, and a sound mind (2 Timothy 1:7).

Live your life today and every day to its fullest by continually reminding yourself that Christ is in you, and you are in Christ. And remember that power, love, and a sound mind rule and reign over you and with you everywhere you go.

To go deeper in finding your true identity in Christ, how to be driven in a healthy way to accomplish God's will in your life, and to understand your ultimate purpose in life, purchase my book, *Identity-Driven Purpose*. It is available on Amazon.

Finally, on the following pages, I have listed all the promises of God that we studied in this book. It might be helpful to come to this section of the book as a review when things in life may not be going your way, and you need to be reminded of how much God loves you and what He says about you.

Blessings to you!

Randy

I am a child of God.

I am a branch of the true vine and a channel of Christ's life.

I am a friend of Jesus.

I am justified and redeemed.

My old self was crucified with Christ, and I am no longer a slave to sin.

I am not and will not be condemned by God.

I am filled with joy and peace, and I abound in hope.

As a child of God, I am a fellow heir with Christ.

I am accepted by Christ.

In Christ Jesus, I have wisdom, righteousness, sanctification, and redemption.

My body is a temple of the Holy Spirit who dwells in me.

I am sealed with the Holy Spirit that was promised to me.

I am joined to the Lord and am one spirit with Him.

God leads me in triumph with Christ and in the knowledge of Christ.

The hardening of my mind and the veiling of my eyes have been removed in Christ.

I am a new creature in Christ.

I have become the righteousness of God in Christ.

I have been made one with all who are in Christ Jesus.

As an heir of God, I am free from the traps of this world.

I have been set free in Christ.

I am blessed with every spiritual blessing in the heavenly places.

I am chosen, holy, and blameless before God.

I am forgiven by the grace of Christ.

Because of Jesus, I am God's possession.

Because of God's mercy and love, I am saved and made alive with Christ.

Because I am raised up with Christ, I have been given His authority.

I am seated in the heavenly places with Christ.

I am God's workmanship created to produce good works.

I am brought near to God by the blood of Christ.

I am a member of Christ's body and a partaker of His promise.

I have boldness and confident access to God through faith in Christ.

I am a new man/woman who is righteous and holy.

I am a citizen of heaven.

The peace of God guards my heart and mind.

God supplies all my needs.

I am made complete in Christ.

My life is hidden with Christ in God.

Christ is my life, and I will be revealed with Him in glory.

I am filled with mercy, kindness, humility, gentleness, and patience.

God loves me.

## OTHER BOOKS BY RANDY VALENTINE

# IDENTITY-
# DRIVEN
# PURPOSE

Transform Your Life
and the
Lives of Those Around You

Randy Valentine

Available on Amazon

Made in the USA
Columbia, SC
11 September 2022

66725476R00059